CAROLYN

Journey to Joy

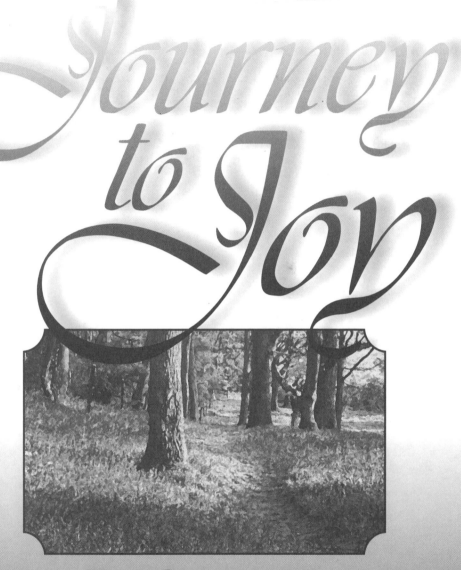

HOW GOD CAN FILL
THE EMPTY PLACES
OF YOUR HEART

REVIEW AND HERALD® PUBLISHING ASSOCIATION
HAGERSTOWN, MD 21740

Copyright © 1997 by Review and Herald® Publishing Association
International copyright secured

The author assumes full responsibility for the accuracy of all
facts and quotations as cited in this book.

Scripture quotations marked NASB are from the *New American
Standard Bible,* © The Lockman Foundation 1960, 1962, 1963, 1968,
1971, 1972, 1973, 1975, 1977.
Texts credited to NIV are from the *Holy Bible, New International
Version.* Copyright © 1973, 1978, 1984, International Bible Society.
Used by permission of Zondervan Bible Publishers.
Bible texts credited to NRSV are from the New Revised Standard
Version of the Bible, copyright © 1989 by the Division of Christian
Education of the National Council of the Churches of Christ in the U.S.A.
Used by permission.

This book was
Edited by Jeannette R. Johnson
Designed by Patricia S. Wegh
Cover photo by Tony Stone
Typeset: 11/12 Galliard

PRINTED IN U.S.A.

01 00 99 98 97   5 4 3 2 1

R&H Cataloging Service
Rathbun, Carolyn, 1944-
    Journey to joy: how God can fill
the empty places of your heart.

    1. Spiritual life.   2. Women-religious life.
3. Joy and sorrow.   4. Self-improvement.
I. Title.

248.843

ISBN 0-8280-1251-2

DEDICATION

For LaVerne and Lucile Roth . . .
who are not just Dad and Mom, but also the first two beautiful people
I ever knew.

Contents

PREFACE

IN PURSUIT OF ALICE

*Why is it that one can never think of the past
without wanting to go back?*
—*C. S. Lewis*

When I first saw her in the store, sitting on a high shelf, I suddenly knew what had been missing from my life all these years. She—the flaxen-haired doll in the blue gingham dress—had been missing! For the first time in my 5-year-old existence, I experienced a cold, black void that only she could fill. As if by mental telepathy, she communicated her name to me: Alice, like a beautiful character from a make-believe story.

Quickly I located my father in the tool aisle of the five-and-dime store and begged him to come see Alice.

No, he would not buy her for me, but he would start giving me an allowance—25 cents a week. I was ecstatic! He gave me the first installment right there on the spot.

"You can save this, or you can spend it. It's your choice."

I raced back to the toy aisle and anxiously looked up to see how much Alice cost. My heart sank. Six dollars and 50 cents.

"Is that what you want to buy?" my father asked, coming up behind me.

"Yes," I answered solemnly.

"Well," he said, "it looks to me like you'll have to save your allowance for a few weeks."

Closing a fist around my shiny quarter, I wandered through the aisles as Daddy completed his tool shopping.

H'mmm. Twenty-five cents would buy five packs of gum. Or an apple-sized red rubber ball. Or a five-feather Indian headdress. None of which I had ever wanted before. Then, hardly believing what I was doing, I picked up the Indian headdress and marched it to the checkout counter. By the time we'd driven the eight blocks home, the red feather had fallen out of the cardboard casing. Soon the yellow one came out, and the blue one broke in half. By evening my younger brother and the dog had taken care of the remaining green and orange feathers. I was sick at heart, and the void that only Alice could fill was still there.

The next Sunday morning, after receiving my second quarter, I suggested that the family drive down to the five-and-dime store to look in on Alice. I came away with the red rubber ball. By daybreak Monday morning our Boston terrier had chewed off large hunks of red, and the ball didn't bounce in a straight line ever again.

When Dad called us into the living room the third week to pass out our allowances, I burst into tears and flung myself into his arms.

"I can't save it!" I sobbed. "I want to, but I can't!"

"Well," he said, drawing me into his lap, "we could keep your allowance in my top dresser drawer, or we could put it in Mother's purse."

I had never thought of doing those things! Why, they told me, I could even have a jar from the kitchen and keep my allowance on top of my *own* dresser. Or—get this—Daddy said I could keep it with *his* money at the bank downtown. I knew he was a powerful man, but I didn't know he could get all the people at the Bank of America in Lodi, California, to help me save my allowance. These amazing options overwhelmed me!

Laughing all the way to the toy store

Six and half months later (having coped all that time with my inner emptiness until I could hold in my arms the beautiful doll as my own), I had finally saved enough money to buy Alice.

Except that I didn't buy her.

You see, on that particular Sunday, with both hands clutching the jar containing $6.50 in quarters, I walked headlong into . . . my first sale. Yes! The five-and-dime store was having a sale on twin baby dolls! Although the twins had only bows taped to their bald rubber heads instead of golden-yellow yarn hair, each *did* have a change of diapers, an undershirt, a bottle, and its own patch of flannel blanket. Two dolls for the price of one—plus all those accessories. This was beyond my wildest budgetary expectations!

As I rode the eight blocks home from the five-and-dime, the fair-haired Alice was a quickly fading memory. Curled up in the back seat, cradling a pink-blanketed bundle in one arm and a blue-blanketed bundle in the other, I proudly gazed into the two vacant painted-on faces of "the twins" and was satisfied. My "inner void" had been filled to overflowing.

No, life wasn't always perfect ever after, for mothering didn't come naturally. Once, Blue Twin lost a toe to the dog before I could snatch its plastic body to safety. Another time I carelessly left Pink Twin outside in my brother's red wagon—in the rain. Shortly after that her rosy lips began to chip off in pinhead-sized chunks, and she had to be put in the "hospital" with pneumonia. Pink Twin eventually recovered, and both the twins lived to a ripe old age.

What are *you* missing?

In a manner of speaking, this book, *Journey to Joy,* is an elaboration of "The Alice Story."

First, identifying the void, loss, deficiency, or inadequacy in one's life. (I felt a loneliness in my life without Alice.) Second, taking that emptiness to the heavenly Father to discover His options for filling that void. (I asked my father for the necessary money, and then he helped me save it for the eventual purchase.) And finally, realizing that our heavenly Parent remains close by, encouraging us to use responsibly His gifts to us. (Though I wanted to treat my twin babies well, I often needed reminders and pointers from my parents on how to be a responsible "mother.")

Because I have yet to meet the girl or woman who believes she is truly beautiful, I have chosen "beauty" as a metaphor for that missing element of joy in one's life. For some, this element might be financial stability; for others, a happier marriage or a more fulfilling job or a man. And for still others, that missing "thing" might be healing for abuse suffered in childhood, the loss of a loved one, or some other deeply scarring trauma.

Filling the void

For many of us, even those with Christian backgrounds, I believe that missing "element" to be Jesus—as He *really* wants to be in our lives. I believe He wants to infuse us and make us over with all the beauty we can possibly bear this side of heaven. Only when our primary pursuit is directed toward the heart of God can we have even half a chance at making sense out of any loss or ongoing pain. The organization of this book reflects my belief.

Part I, "The Beauty of Uncertainty" (chapters 1-7), examines unexpected loss and a coming to terms with it. It begins with my earliest pursuit of beauty (an attempt to be a parade majorette), introduces the motif of a lost baton, and explores biblical principles regarding the relationship between hardship and hope. I share, in part, a devastation of my own and a few subsequent steps in the long journey back toward healing.

Part II, "The Magnificent Makeover (in Four Easy Steps)" (chapters 8-15), explores possible reasons behind our sometimes obsessive pursuit of "beauty" and then proposes the solution to life's "cosmetic" needs.

Part III, "Portrait of a Beautiful Woman" (chapters 16-25), describes what a woman of beauty "looks" like and what she does, on a daily basis, to *maintain*—yes, and even improve!—her Magnificent Makeover.

And finally . . .

Like the demoniac on the Galilean shore, I am neither a theologian nor a preacher, merely a grateful recipient of unmerited grace. When that newly healed man pleaded to join Christ's entourage, the Lord gently gave him another commission: tell "how much the Lord has done for you, and how he has had mercy on you" (Mark 5:19, NIV).

At the most basic level, this book is my simple attempt to do just that.

Part One

THE BEAUTY
OF UNCERTAINTY

CHAPTER 1

THE LOST BATON

"Hope" is the thing with feathers
That perches in the soul,
And sings the tune without the words,
And never stops—at all.
—Emily Dickinson

The sight that launched me on my earliest pursuit of beauty was that majorette twirling a silver baton. Forgetting to sip my grape soda, I sat on the hot curb beside my sweaty little brother, just watching. That lovely, high-stepping creature suddenly tossed the sparkling scepter of silver up into the air. As the baton rose to the top of the Foster Freeze sign, she kept marching in time to the snare drums. Then the whirling baton streaked back toward her. Still marching in time—and smiling—she snatched it just before it hit the pavement.

Wow!

And all this was only leading up to the one-handed cartwheel she did before throwing herself down in an arched-back split, while holding the magic baton theatrically aloft. And she was *still* smiling.

That dazzling performance at the head of the Lodi, California, Grape Festival parade instilled a new resolve in my 6-year-old heart: I would become a baton-twirling majorette in a parade.

Seven weeks later, on a scorching autumn afternoon, I followed my parents into the five-and-dime store. There I exchanged a small jar containing six weeks' worth of allowance (minus tithe) for my first symbol of beauty—an aluminum alloy baton.

Once home I rushed to the dress-up drawer, where my mother tossed her worn-out petticoats, and selected a white satin petticoat with only one rip in the side. As its cool smoothness slipped over my perspiring skin and fell in ripples about my ankles, I felt instantly transformed into a beautiful majorette and started to march in place.

How the neighbors must have laughed, watching that silly little girl marching up and down the driveway, wearing her mother's old hitched-up slip, and clumsily waving that cheap toy about while singing her favorite Sabbath school song.

Sadly, my dream of someday leading the Grape Festival parade was shattered by one of the first uncertainties to come into my life. A short time later, during my family's move to a new house, I lost my baton.

This early-life interest in baton twirling probably explains why I was so fascinated by the story of a high school drum major in Ventura, California. This young man had worked for years perfecting his baton-twirling abilities and most certainly must have hoped to bring honor to his school during that city's annual parade. How shocked he must have been, therefore, during the parade when, in the midst of a spectacular toss of his silver baton, the brilliantly spinning blur suddenly hit a power cable . . . and melted . . . and blacked out 10 city blocks . . . and put the local radio station off the air. The resulting power box explosion started a raging grass fire.[1] Talk about losing one's baton!

Lost dreams

Have you ever lost a silver baton? Have you ever experienced one of those unexpected, unfair uncertainties that mar life's beauty and strangle your dreams?

One summer afternoon a few years ago I stood before the knife drawer in my kitchen. An emotional anguish throbbed through my entire body; I had only recently become aware that our marriage had been irreparably damaged. Having just completed an emergency medical technician certification, I had a fairly accurate idea between which two ribs I could slip a blade and penetrate the heart, bringing an end to its intense pain. My questionable mental state that hot July afternoon assured me the act would be justifiably merciful.

At that moment our 19-year-old son began pounding on a drum set he kept in his room. That seemed to be his way of coping with our unexpected family crisis. How could I deprive him of a mother during this personal catastrophe unfolding in his life? I was sane enough to realize that even this supreme love for my only child might not be strong enough just then to win out over the brown-handled knife with the serrated four-inch blade. In a tortuous act of will, I turned on my heel, grabbed the keys to one of our cars, and backed down the long driveway.

The car sped down winding mountain roads I'd never seen before while I sobbed out angry phrases of prayer to a God who seemed "unable to come to the phone right now, but please leave a message." Driving like a woman possessed, I noticed how each approaching curve teased me to press harder on the accelerator, daring me never to turn the steering wheel again.

Sometime toward the end of that first hour of the longest trip of my life, I found myself driving through an unfamiliar town. Suddenly, as if from the sky, they appeared—gigantic red words burning through my grief and exploding into my benumbed brain: "Midsummer Clearance Clothing Bonanza!"

I downshifted into third gear.

"Last day of sale!"

My car made an abrupt U-turn.

"Prices slashed up to 70 percent on most items!"

I screeched to a halt next to the handicapped parking spot and did what I had to do. Putting my untimely end on hold, I marched into that clothing store as if it were my last shopping trip on earth. The tables, heaped high with discounted items, set my pulse to racing.

One hour later I emerged from that clothing store somewhere in the San Joaquin Valley with the will to live—at least long enough to get some good, practical use out of the all-cotton, cable-knit, bleeding-heart red sweater I'd just nabbed at a killer price. The car I was driving instinctively pulled into my parents' driveway in southern California—350 miles down the road.

Twenty months later, after 23 years of faith in the beauty of a Christian marriage and in a God who, in my opinion, should have been more responsible for keeping it intact, the unthinkable had taken place. And when the divorce papers arrived, the only person I had to share them with was the mid-40ish, haggard-looking woman staring back at me from the bathroom mirror. Her hollow eyes reflected an inner hollowness quickly filling with disappointment in—and confusion about— a silent God.

Why?

A person's reaction to uncertainty can take several forms. For most of us the immediate reaction is almost a need to know *why* we lost that cherished baton. For me, those silent screams began immediately. Over and over I demanded answers: *Why? Why this? Why now? Why me?*

Job wrestled with these why questions; he also wrestled with God's silence. "But if I go to the east, he is not there; if I go to the west, I do not find him. When he is at work in the north, I do not see him; when he turns to the south, I catch no glimpse of him" (Job 23:8, 9, NIV). J.B., the Job character in Archibald MacLeish's contemporary play about this Bible patriarch, cries out:

> "What I *can't* bear is the blindness—
> Meaninglessness—the numb blow
> Fallen in the stumbling night."[2]

Has God ever been silent about a lost baton of yours? Is He being silent about one right now? If so, I invite you to keep that uncertainty of yours in mental view as together we begin our *journey to joy!*

[1] Nigel Blundell, ed., *World's Greatest Mistakes* (London: Octopus Books Ltd., 1982), p. 21.

[2] Archibald MacLeish, *J.B.* (Boston: Houghton-Mifflin Co., 1956), p. 108.

CHAPTER 2

BUT LOOK AT WHAT'S LEFT!

the sacred glen
the strong pine air
alone on skis—
a dream, a prayer

i'd hoped to stay
beneath that sky—
but snow's now gone
and so am i.
—Carolyn Rathbun

We often worry about how we look when we're with people, right? Well, there's one activity of my life in which personal appearance is the last thing with which I am concerned. That activity is caving. I am a card-carrying member of the National Speleological Society.

While spelunking a few months ago with a small group of people in a wild cave near Grants Pass, Oregon, I waded through calf-deep water and crawled through muddy tunnels in order to visit several subterranean rooms. These rooms reputedly contained beautiful crystal formations.

Bob, our trip leader, led the three of us into some rooms whose ancient formations had suffered a substantial amount of vandalism. As we arrived in each room, we three, all rather ecology-minded, would groan as we looked at the remaining stalactite stubs on the ceiling and the shattered calcite shards on the cavern floor. But Bob, who is hopelessly sanguine, seemed almost not to hear us, for he was already ecstatically exclaiming, "Look at what's left!"

It wasn't until the third or fourth time that Bob insisted we take our eyes off the destruction and focus on remaining formations that I actually began to hear what he was saying. And he was right! Exquisite beauty surrounded me when I chose to "look at what's left."

Much of my personal reading since that summer day in front of the knife drawer has been an attempt to look at what's left.

What *is* left, anyway?

First of all, wanting to understand what had happened to love in my life—what it had been and what it hadn't been—I "camped" for a time in 1 Corinthians 13 and, of course, in the inevitable thirteenth verse: "And now these three remain: faith, hope and love" (NIV).

Look at what's left. Certainly not love! Faith? Huh! Faith was gurgling down the drain like so much dirty dishwater. And hope? You've got to be kidding! Besides, I'd always assumed hope was just another name for faith. All I could remember Christ ever talking about were love and faith. God is love. Have the faith of a little child. Faith the size of a mustard seed moves mountains. And after performing some miracle, Christ would send off the healed person with a blessing such as "Thy faith hath made thee whole."

I found no story in which the Lord patted a cleansed leper on the head and pronounced, "Go in peace, for thy *hope* hath made thee whole." *So what*, I wondered, is *the difference between hope and faith?*

In a state of confusion, this English teacher went to a trusted friend of hers, the dictionary, to find the difference between faith and hope. Among other definitions, the dictionary defines *faith* as "a confident belief in the truth, value, or trustworthiness of a person, idea, or thing." *Hope,* on the other hand, is defined as a "wish or desire accompanied by confident expectation." *

Simply put, the difference between faith and hope is that faith involves a *belief* in something or someone, while hope involves a *wish* or *desire* for something with *expectation of fulfillment.*

Well, that made sense, because although my *belief* in God's leading at that point in my life was definitely shaken, I certainly retained a strong *desire* to get out of the painful present (along with a weak *expectation* that somehow, someday, I wouldn't be hurting so much).

"Desires" in the Old Testament

Actually, I did recall a text that speaks about desires: "Delight thyself also in the Lord; and he shall give thee the desires of thine heart" (Ps. 37:4). Was the author of this text suggesting that God honors not only our *belief*, but also our *desires?*

Psalm 10:17 states, "Lord, thou hast heard the desire of the humble," while Psalm 145:19 promises, "He will fulfil the desire of them that fear him." Other writers of the Scriptures sprinkle occasional accounts of God being touched, not only by His people's faith, but also by their hopes. He sometimes even granted His children's desires when He knew the wishes He was granting would not be used wisely.

When the children of Israel complained about the manna that God had so faithfully supplied and expressed a desire for flesh food (Num. 11), God sent them quail, even when the resulting intemperate eating caused widespread disease and death. And when the Israelites begged for a temporal king a few years later (1 Sam. 8), God granted that desire, too—even after prophetic warning that resulting pride and greed in the Hebrew monarchy would eventually lead to Israel's downfall.

A different perspective

These last two biblical examples were helpful to me because they point out that because of His omniscience, God's perspective on my situation might be much different than my perspective on my situation.

A second grader illustrated this difference in perspectives one day when she approached me during lunch break.

"You're Ms. Rathbun, the new teacher, aren't you!" she asserted, nodding her head vigorously.

"Yes, I am. Who are you?"

"I'm Ashley," she answered confidently, "and you teach my big sister, Samantha."

"Samantha? In the seventh grade? Samantha is your sister?" I could now see the resemblance of this little brown-eyed blond to the studious Samantha. "I just love Samantha!" I exclaimed. "She is *so* sweet!"

A look of irritation came over Ashley's face as she first paused and then responded, "H'mmm . . . that's what I've heard."

Ashley and I obviously had very different perspectives on Samantha. And God may have a very different perspective from ours regarding our uncertainties.

American Heritage Dictionary, Second College Edition.

CHAPTER 3

THE STRESSFUL WAIT

Patience is a lonely friend
Whose company is dull,
A solitary voice within
To hold one back—where fools rush in.
—Carolyn Rathbun

All right, so a few Old Testament writers tell us that God was aware of His children's desires and hopes. I was curious, however, if New Testament writers recorded anyone with something to say about this topic. It turned out they certainly did! And the speakers and writers were individuals who had experienced plenty of uncertainty in their own lives—Jesus, John, and Paul.

Mark 11:24 relates that after performing the miracle of the barren fig tree, Christ says to Peter and the other disciples, "Therefore I say unto you, What things soever ye desire, when ye pray, believe that ye receive them, and ye shall have them."

John the Beloved, in instructing his readers how to pray according to God's will, promises, "And if we know that he hear us, whatsoever we ask, we know that we have the petitions that we desired of him" (1 John 5:15).

And Paul explains the relationship between uncertainty and hope. He states in Romans 5 that tribulations (hard experiences, uncertainties) bring first patience, which turns into experience, which turns into . . . yes, hope. He then adds, "Hope maketh not ashamed" (verse 5). The *New American Standard Bible* words this thought as "And hope does not disappoint."

Hope doesn't disappoint

Once I read an incredible story of someone who risked having his desires disappointed, but chose to be hopeful anyway. His name was Octavio Guillen. At the turn of the century, while living in Mexico City, Octavio met and fell madly in love with Adriana Martinez. Within two years Octavio had convinced Adriana to be his fiancée. Friends and acquaintances were thrilled, concurring that the two young people made a lovely couple. But Octavio, it seems, couldn't convince Adriana to marry him as soon as he had hoped. However, his hopeful waiting finally paid off. For in 1969 Adriana finally cast her lot with Octavio and married him. They were both 82 years old and had been engaged for 67 years.[1]

The stress of waiting

But that was Octavio's long wait not meeting with disappointment. What about yours—and mine?

Oswald Chambers writes, "If our hopes seem to be experiencing disappointment right now, it simply means that they are being purified. Every hope or dream of the human mind will be fulfilled if it is noble and of God."[2] Chambers concludes, "But one of the greatest stresses in life is the stress of waiting for God."[3]

Bible stories about people suffering through the stressful wait on God provide valuable insights. One, in particular, caught my attention. John recounts how Jesus and His disciples were passing through a town in which a blind man pleaded for healing. Christ appeared to delay the healing process. "He spat on the ground," John records, "and made clay of the spittle, and he anointed the eyes of the blind man with the clay" (John 9:6). Then Jesus told him to go wash in the Pool of Siloam.

Now tell me, don't you think it would be stressful to go to the great Miracle Worker, expecting to be healed, only to have Him smear spit-moistened mud on your eyes while you stood there, completely helpless? Don't you think it would be stressful to be ordered, in front of a crowd as if you were a child, to go wash your face? And this you could accomplish only after groping your way to the public well?

But the blind man chose to persevere in his stressful wait, and he received his sight.

Washing at the pool

Thinking about how Christ handled this particular healing, I've wondered if God doesn't sometimes allow the resolution of our uncertainties to take longer than we want in order to give us time to visit the Pool of Siloam to wash—to wash away an unforgiving spirit . . . or pride . . . or lack of self-control . . . or the blame we might have placed on someone else for choices that we made. Maybe it takes time to wash away the results of impurity from the past so that we will have the assurance of a wholesome and happy future.

Perhaps God doesn't allow clear vision in the outward world so that we can see more clearly when we look inward. Paul reminds us that we are renewed when "we look not at the things which are seen, but at the things which are not seen: for the things which are seen are temporal; but the things which are not seen are eternal" (2 Cor. 4:18).

Through God's eyes

Or, as Bob, my cave guide, illustrated, maybe our stressful wait has to do with looking at what's left as God helps us see through His eyes.

What do you have left, Moses, now that you've lost your right to the throne and have a price on your murderous head? A worn-smooth sheepherder's rod? or a divine instrument that parts seas and brings water gushing from dry rock?

You, destitute widow (2 Kings 4), with your sons about to be sold into slavery to pay your debts, what do you have left? A few drops of grease in your skillet? or a supermarket running a gigantic special on cooking oil because of divine overstocking?

Little boy, there! What's left in your lunch? Five hard biscuits and a couple strips of fish jerky? or a feast for 5,000 people, plus 12 bushel basketfuls left over?

And you, what do you have left?

---

[1] Stephen Pile, ed., *The Incomplete Book of Failures* (New York: E. P. Dutton, 1979), p. 152.

[2] Oswald Chambers, in James Reimann, ed., *My Utmost for His Highest* (Nashville: Discovery House Publishers, 1982), Feb. 22 entry.

[3] *Ibid.*

CHAPTER 4

MARRYING THE LEFTOVERS

*Those who hopefully wait for Me
will not be put to shame.*
—Isaiah 49:23, NASB

One year a delightful foreign exchange student enrolled in my British literature class. Although the schoolwork was well above his head, he begged to be able to have the same homework as the rest of the seniors. One day he struggled through an oral report on a British short story he had read. He told it something like this:

"Young man fall in love with three girls. He ask number one favorite girl to marry him. She say, 'Oh, no.' He ask number two favorite girl to marry him. She say, 'Oh . . . no.' Young man look at number three. He say, 'Oh, no! Nothing for me to do now but marry the leftovers.'"

What follows is a three-part minidocumentary entitled "Women Who Married the Leftovers."

Part 1

Part 1 of "Women Who Married the Leftovers" recounts the "Saga of Sarah." Married to Abraham, a man of faith, Sarah still felt the stress of waiting for God. In fact, she felt so much stress while waiting for a divinely promised son she insisted that her husband sleep with another woman. (In my book, that's stress spelled with a capital S!)

But finally Sarah, wrinkled, stooped, and light-years beyond child-bearing age, chose to "marry the leftovers." The leftovers for her were to stick with her old man in front of a childless hearth and hang tight with the status quo. Instead of compounding their misery any more by second-guessing God, Sarah patiently waited out this time of uncertainty in the hope of God's promise.

Then, as one little girl explained the miracle, "Abraham and Sarah . . . learned how to waltz."[1] And they certainly must have, for one morning, with great excitement, Sarah described to Abraham the faint tremors of new life nudging the insides of her shriveled belly. And Sarah, who had married the leftovers, gave birth to the long-promised son, Isaac, whose descendants became as the stars of the heavens and the sands of the sea.

Part 2

Part 2 of the documentary "Women Who Married the Leftovers" portrays the real-life struggles of "Naomi, the Wandering Widow." You may recall how at one point Naomi was tempted to change her name to Mara, or "bitterness."

Have you ever been tempted to be bitter? Hebrews 4:15 tells us that Jesus was "in all points tempted like as we are." In addition to the daily temptations that would normally come to mind, don't you think that during times of emotional misery our sensitive Saviour was also tempted (as Naomi was or you or I have been) to lose faith, to discard hope, to doubt that His heavenly Father was with Him?

We have only to recall Christ's words in the Garden of Gethsemane (Mark 14:36) and on the cross (Mark 15:34) in order to answer that question. Of course He was tempted! And on those very points. You see, one reason God hates the suffering in *our* lives so much is that He remembers the suffering in *His*—and how desperately it hurts.

Naomi's stressful wait began when a famine parched Israel. She accompanied her family into exile, hoping to find greener pastures in Moab. Soon, however, Naomi was left a widow with two young sons in this foreign land. Time passed, and Naomi eventually heaved two great sighs of relief when her boys each found a nice Moabite girl to marry. Soon happy grandchildren would cheer her barren hearth. But 10 short years after her arrival in Moab, both sons died, leaving no offspring.

Now three widows lived in the same house, pooling "their meager resources to eke out a living, . . . bound . . . by their mutual love for the memories of the same dead men."[2] In her book *Just a Sister Away* Renita Weems points out that at this point in Naomi's life "no angel of mercy came. . . . No divine messenger offered counsel. . . . No God came with words of wisdom and assurance."[3]

Marry the leftovers. The leftovers for Naomi were the remaining hope that though she had lost everything and everyone dear to her, she might at least be able to die in the land of her birth and of her God. Back to Israel she went, accompanied by her ardent and beautiful daughter-in-law, Ruth.

In little leftover Bethlehem God ordained a much lesser miracle than He was to perform centuries later in that same small village. Boaz, an important, kind, and distant relative, chose Ruth as his wife, and in the courtship process redeemed her from potential marriage with a man who really didn't care. Ruth, her redeemer-kinsman husband, and the children they had smothered Naomi with comfort, security, and love for the rest of her days.

Although Naomi had no way of knowing it then, Ruth was to become a great-grandmother of Israel's most famous monarch, King

David, as well as an ancestor in the earthly family tree of our Redeemer-Kinsman, the Son of God.

In *God of the Whirlwind*, his book on Job, Gerald Wheeler states, "While suffering can never be explained or justified, it can be redeemed."[4] Maybe this is just another way of wording the apostle Paul's thought: "And we know that all things work together for good" (Rom. 8:28).

Part 3

Part 3 of "Women Who Married the Leftovers" remains untitled. For the title is your call. You see, Part 3 is about you (and me) and the story each of us has to tell of a lost baton and a stressful wait for God. And although I would like to hear what you did (or are doing) about your leftovers, I suppose, being the one sitting here at the computer, I should continue my story.

---

[1] David Heller, *Just Build the Ark and the Animals Will Come* (New York: Villard Books, 1994), p. 43.

[2] Renita J. Weems, *Just a Sister Away* (San Diego: LuraMedia, 1988), p. 25.

[3] *Ibid.*

[4] Gerald Wheeler, *God of the Whirlwind* (Hagerstown, Md.: Review and Herald Pub. Assn., 1992), p. 155.

CHAPTER 5

HARD HATS AND TOOL BELTS

He who, from zone to zone,
Guides through the boundless sky thy certain flight,
In the long way that I must tread alone,
Will lead my steps aright.
—William Cullen Bryant

My leftovers, after that long drive to southern California following the knife-drawer afternoon, consisted of a poetry journal and being sent off by a concerned father to a total stranger for counseling. At that first session the first question I blurted out was "Will I ever feel happy again?" What I also wanted to ask was "Will I ever hear from God again?"

In giving me practical suggestions for coming to grips with my situation, the counselor emphasized the importance of continued journaling, of crying when I felt like it, and of praying. Experiencing insomnia during that time, I took to long, hard-driving, early-morning walks downtown and back.

On one of those walks I found myself on Brand Street just as rush-hour traffic was at its peak. In the flurry of shopkeepers and business types rushing to their morning responsibilities, I noticed an elderly couple, obvious by their lack of haste. They strolled hand in hand, pausing to look in shop windows. I couldn't help noticing the affection they held for each other. Most of all, I couldn't help noticing that one of my dreams—the one about walking into those sunset years with a lifelong loved one—was dying along with the other dreams.

tried not to

i tried not to
    (from behind my sunglasses
    and writing tablet)
i tried not to
    watch them,
    teetering over sturdy brown canes,

his free hand under her free elbow
steadying her—or himself—
i could not tell since
i tried not to
  look at them
  and put my pen to its tablet
  but it wouldn't write—
  not with the same easy grace
  their aged bodies assumed
  as they ambled past
  in perfect step
  despite the canes—
i tried not to
  notice their moving away like
  two synchronized skaters,
  two wings on a bird,
  two syllables of a word—
  and then
  (behind my sunglasses
  and writing tablet)
i tried not to . . . remember
  being coaxed out of myself once
  being one half of a whole once,
  being close once . . .
  i did remember, but
i tried not to

An overwhelming urge to cry swept over me. My first reaction was
Not here! Not with all these cars going by and professional people passing.
Then I remembered my therapist's advice to cry when I felt like it, because that would promote healing. So, blinded by hot tears and thank-
ful for dark glasses, I staggered uncertainly to the curb and sank down.

The last time I'd sat on a curb was to watch a parade led by a majorette with a silver baton. Now 40 years later, feet in the gutter and
head in my hands, I sat on another curb and wept . . . for the baton I
had lost.

Construction site
When the worst was over, I began taking stock of where I was.
Glancing up through swollen eyelids, I saw a high-rise building in
progress on the other side of the boulevard. Construction workers
swarmed over the scaffolding as they began their new day's work. That
is, all but two workers on the second-story scaffold.

Those two, dressed for a hot summer workday in regulation hard hats, tank tops, and rawhide tool belts, stood silent, looking down at me with expressions of concern—even worry—on their faces. Realizing the small spectacle I must have created by my quiet outburst, I stood up quickly, waved an embarrassed "I'm OK," and took off down the sidewalk. But a touch of inner warmth welled up inside me from the respectful concern I had just received from two of Daly Construction's finest. Heaving a weary sigh toward heaven, and assuming the celestial answering machine was *not* on, I left this absurd little message: *God, what I think I need about now is a job on a construction site.*

Little did I realize that not only was heaven's answering machine on, but Someone was listening—and already preparing to return my call.

"The phone's for you!" Mother's voice carried down the hallway two days later. The individual on the other end of the line was a long-time family friend. Currently an administrator with a large hospital in the Los Angeles area, she was calling to offer me a part-time office management job for just a month, and I could call my own hours. Thinking it over briefly, I accepted on the spot.

"Great!" she responded with characteristic enthusiasm. "Now that you've accepted, I'll tell you where you'll be working. We're in the middle of a $3 million renovation and building project, adding a new wing to our hospital." She hesitated briefly before continuing. "Carolyn, I hope you don't have a problem with this, but you'll be helping to run the main office down on the construction site."

My body went numb as I clumsily replaced the telephone receiver on its hook. "Lord God in heaven," I gasped, "I was only kidding!"

The next four weeks, in addition to being issued my own McCarthy Construction hard hat, I worked as assistant office manager for five architects, who were among the most respectful gentlemen I have ever met. I also survived running a few errands out on the site, as well as the topping-off celebration.

The other construction site

While He had me working for McCarthy Construction that month, God gave me a hard hat and a tool belt, too. He wanted my cooperation and participation on a new renovation project of His own: strengthening my tottering pillar of faith and clearing away the collapsed walls of love and trust. The next time their establishment would be more firmly grounded than before, since God was securing them all on a new foundation—hope.

As He did with Job, God never answered my why questions with words. Rather, He answered them with Himself.*

---

*See R. C. Sproul, *The Holiness of God* (Wheaton, Ill.: Tyndale House, 1985), p. 181.

CHAPTER 6

GRACIOUS UNCERTAINTY

*Hope is nothing else than the expectation of those things
which faith has believed to have been truly promised by God.*
—John Calvin

*If only for this life we have hope in Christ,
we are to be pitied more than all men.*
—Paul of Tarsus

None of us is unique in the long walk though the cold, foggy tunnel of uncertainty. "Uncertainty haunts each one of us," writes Jerry Westfall. "There are no guarantees that life will be easy and we will live in comfort and security. . . . I have the same challenge that . . . you face," he continues. "That is the challenge to trust God in the face of uncertainty."[1]

I once had the privilege of hearing Dave Dravecky speak. A former pitcher with the San Francisco Giants, Dravecky battled cancer in his pitching arm, surviving several surgeries. He returned to his beloved sport, only to shatter that same arm during a game being aired on national television. In his autobiography, *Comeback*, he writes, "The hardest part of the last two years has been the uncertainty. I had to learn to do what was within my grasp, one day at a time, and leave control of the rest trustingly to God."[2]

Remember that uncertainty of yours that I invited you to keep within mental view? That illness . . . difficult person . . . horrific memory from the past . . . decision you wish you (or someone else) hadn't made . . . financial uncertainty . . . addiction . . . child making hurtful choices . . . beloved parent struggling with the unjust ravages of aging . . . or simply an indescribable loneliness you might be feeling, no matter what your marital status . . .

That uncertainty of yours—with any accompanying confusion, rage, pain, or ugliness—matters as much to God as did Sarah's infertility and Naomi's multiple losses. The Redeemer-Kinsman does have a redemptive plan to bring beauty out of your uncertainty.

"Certainty," wrote Oswald Chambers, "is the mark of the commonsense life—gracious uncertainty is the mark of the spiritual life. To be certain of God means that we are uncertain in all our ways, not knowing what tomorrow may bring. . . . As soon as we abandon ourselves to God and do the task He has placed closest to us, He begins to fill our lives with surprises. . . . Leave everything to Him and it will be gloriously and graciously uncertain how He will come in—but you can be certain that He will come."[3]

Having just passed the half-century mark in my life, I look back at those times of uncertainty and see, more and more, God's working in, through, and in spite of those uncertainties. And to think that I even wondered, at times, if He was hearing my prayers! With gratitude, I can now refer to each time of uncertainty as a "Jacob experience."

Jacob, a lonely, defeated cheat, lying out on the hard ground in some foreign wilderness, saw no divine plan in his uncertainty—one he'd brought upon himself. Yet the God of unconditional love gave Jacob an unexpected glimpse of Himself in the dream of an angel-laden ladder stretching from heaven to earth. Jacob awoke and exclaimed, "Surely the Lord is in this place; and I knew it not" (Gen. 28:16).

Andrew Young, in referring to his own uncertainties, observed, "What may seem accidental or even tragic at the time of occurrence turns out to be, in retrospect, just one more development in a continuously unfolding, marvelously meaningful plan for one's life."[4]

One author notes that "Hope is rooted in God's faithfulness."[5] Everything else is sinking sand.

Giver of batons

Most of us have lost at least one silver baton during life's parade. Do you know what my greatest hope is? It is to stand one day in a little huddle with God, along with Sarah and Naomi—glorious in our gowns of satin light—and listen as He reveals to each of us how He went about fulfilling our deepest desires, wildest wishes, and highest hopes. Then we three women will probably start to move on for further exploration of the Holy City.

Knowing He is so capable of those "surprises" Oswald Chambers mentions, I wouldn't put it past the Lord to say something like "Psst, Carolyn! Could you stay with Me a minute or two? I just want you to know that something I haven't forgotten about is . . . *this.*"

And from out of somewhere—thin air, for all I know—my Creator and Source of hope pulls out . . . a silver baton! He places it in my hands. Speechless, I stare at it while somewhere out of the universal distance a bass drum begins to beat.

"Go ahead," the Lord encourages.

"Lord," I protest, "You know I never really knew how to twirl a baton. I just waved it around and marched to my favorite Sabbath school song."

"What song?" He asks.

"You know—the one I kept singing even after I lost that first baton, the one that kept me marching through danger in the mission field, the one You helped me sing through two back surgeries and a divorce, the one that brings me through one uncertainty after another."

"Sing it again," He quietly requests, "for Me—with your new baton. Remember that My strength is made perfect in weakness."

The little song

So I start singing the little song that never seems to wear out, while I awkwardly try to twirl the baton:

> "Jesus loves me! this I know,
> For the Bible tells me so;
> Little ones to Him belong,
> They are weak, but He is strong."
> (This was always my favorite line.)
> "Yes, Jesus loves me!
> Yes, Jesus loves me!
> Yes, Jesus loves me!
> The Bible tells me so."[6]

As I end my song, I notice that Naomi and Sarah have turned around and are staring, their mouths hanging open. The Lord is looking at me with a mixture of love and, well, pity.

"May I?" He asks gently. I hand Him the baton, and He starts twirling it. Sparkles, the color of every hue in the rainbow, shower gloriously everywhere. "Watch this," He says modestly, and with an effortless toss throws our baton up into the sky. As it ascends higher and higher, gushing streams of miniature comets from both ends, the Fourth of July explodes throughout the universe.

With unspeakable gratitude I look at my Lord. My pursuit of beauty has come to an end. I have found it. I am looking it full in its radiant face. I now understand that during those long, stressful waits He was molding the desires of my heart to fit the desires of His heart—for me.

Our eyes meet, and I know what I'm supposed to do. Getting into position, just as I saw that majorette do in the Lodi Grape Festival parade, I fearlessly watch the baton spin back toward me. With a confidence born of expectation that has been fulfilled, I call out, "I got it!" and snatch the silver baton just before it hits the street of gold. I do a one-handed cartwheel and land in a perfect split. And I'm *smiling* the whole time.

The Lord, who created—and redeemed—you and me for His own happiness, begins to chuckle. "A parade's just starting out there," He says, gesturing toward the heavens, "and [I hold my breath] I need someone to lead it."

From far away, percussive rhythms of a thousand snare drums pound new blood through my veins. Then, like a spinning propeller that I'm effortlessly passing from one hand to the other, the baton begins to lift me. On a beam of light radiating from my Saviour's face, the silver baton and I shoot through the heavens. Giddy on glory, I ride the mighty waves of His laughter past a billion outlying stars along the Milky Way toward my first celestial parade.

[1] Jerry Westfall, *Enough Is Enough* (San Francisco: Zondervan, 1993), p. 126.

[2] Dave Dravecky, as quoted in Westfall, p. 126.

[3] Oswald Chambers, in *My Utmost for His Highest,* Apr. 29 entry.

[4] Andrew Young, as quoted in "Possibilities," *A Way Out of No Way: The Spiritual Memoirs of Andrew Young* (Garden Grove, Calif.: Robert Schuler Ministries), p. 13.

[5] Westfall, p. 66.

[6] Anna B. Warner, "Jesus Loves Me," *The Seventh-day Adventist Hymnal* (Hagerstown, Md.: Review and Herald Pub. Assn., 1985), No. 190.

CHAPTER 7

PURSUING THE BEAUTY . . . OF UNCERTAINTY

Hope is faith holding out its hand.
—Author Unknown

We live in a sinful world whose final days are numbered. One has only to compare current world events with Bible prophecies to draw this conclusion. In my heart of hearts, I am convinced that Jesus is coming—and soon—to bring an end to all suffering.

In the meantime, we are trapped on Planet Earth. And that means we will live, at least part of the time, with heartbreak and uncertainty. Yet there lives, from the farthest reaches of the universe to the most sheltered place of the heart, a God of hope.

That God has provided the means necessary for us to augment our supply of hope to overflowing, even while we are waiting "down here" for Him to return. Some of these means include the unfolding of certain serrendipitous events in our lives, or through the loving choices of people who care about us. But hope based on just these outward manifestations will not be strong enough to anchor us during the major storms in this life.

The two most abundant sources of hope

The surest means of obtaining and maintaining a hope that will withstand any loss or trauma are, surprisingly, those most accessible to us: prayer and Bible reading. Through the opening of our hearts to the heavenly Parent in prayer—a two-way conversation—we invite Him to move into our souls more intimately and enduringly than any human friend ever could.

And finally, through the openhearted reading of His holy Word we receive a continual increase in understanding about God and how He relates to our personal circumstances. Did you know that one reason the Bible even *exists* is to pour hope into the hearts of its readers? "For everything that was written in the past was written to teach us, so that through endurance and the encouragement of the Scriptures we might have hope" (Rom. 15:4, NIV).

Back to your uncertainty . . .

Remember a few chapters back, when I suggested you keep an uncertainty of yours within mental peripheral vision as we explored the topics of hope and uncertainty? In your mind, would you now turn and stare at your uncertainty? As honestly as possible, identify your greatest wish regarding this uncertainty . . . your deepest desire.

As we close this section, I invite you to take some private moments to tell that desire to God. And I will tell Him mine.

❦ ❦ ❦

> Dear Father, who suffers when we suffer,
>   The stress of waiting is *so* hard.
>   Just now we each have something we want to share
>   with You—and You alone.
>
>   Lord God, we acknowledge that
>   the beauty of any uncertainty,
>   any trial,
>   any loss,
>   is that when we surrender "what is left" to You . . .
>   You transform it into hope itself.
>
>   For You are not only the God of love and faith . . .
>   You are also the God of hope.
>   With You, we leave our desire.
>   In You, we place our hope.
>
>   These things we pray in the name of Jesus . . .
>   the Redeemer of all suffering.
>   Amen.

❦ ❦ ❦

Beautiful woman, the promise God gave to the captive and suffering children of Israel, He gives to you: "There is hope for your future" (Jer. 31:17, NASB).

Part Two

THE MAGNIFICENT MAKEOVER (IN FOUR EASY STEPS)

CHAPTER 8

"MOM! YOUR LEGS!"

Out of the mouth of babes . . .
—Matthew 21:16

One afternoon during our mission stint in central Africa, I slipped into our bedroom to do a few stretching exercises for my weak back. Kent, our 4-year-old son, whom I'd put down for a nap, suddenly pushed open the door. Not used to seeing his mother in anything other than an ankle-length, traditional African dress (much less gym shorts), little Kent stared.

After watching me stretch for a minute or so, the face of my child lit up as it did whenever he thought he'd made a brilliant discovery.

"Mom!" he cried excitedly. "Look at your legs!"

I did.

"Mom, up to your knees your legs look like . . . just regular legs. But after the knees," my darling child continued with a voice full of amazement, "your legs get kinda *big* . . . and *fat*—like the rest of your body!"

Well, at least he'd said that in private. I thanked him for sharing his observation and assumed the subject was now behind us.

The following month our family drove for three hours to enjoy an afternoon at the pool of a posh, high-rise hotel in the capital city. At least 40 international guests, including two very trim-looking flight crews from Belgium's Sabena Airlines, were lounging in the sun. From across the pool my little son watched me self-consciously emerge from the very public dressing room. Then his sweet voice rang out across the water, loud and clear.

"Mom! Your legs!"

Oh, no! Not this again! The African sun grew real hot while I automatically glanced down at my legs (as did everyone else within earshot).

"Oh, Mom," called my son, giggling, "your legs just *crack me up!*"

Bigger is better (we wish) . . .

This incident might have devastated me forever if I hadn't been able, a couple hours later, to fade back into the local culture where "bigger is better."

In fact, the first time an African friend said to me, "How fat you're getting!" I didn't know how to respond—except mumble something about eating too much. Then I rushed home and jumped on the scales. However, after I understood the culture better, I learned to react to such *compliments* more gracefully. "Oh, do you really think so?" I'd reply. "You're not just saying that, are you?"

Upon returning to the United States after nine years of teaching in African communities, where one is accepted no matter what one's weight, I was amazed at the pressure exerted on people in this country to be concerned about their appearance. Almost as soon as I returned, assertive Avon and Mary Kay representatives began pressuring me to get my makeup act together, and everyone seemed to be on some kind of a diet.

Perhaps this pressure explains why dieting has turned into a $33 billion a year industry.[1] Aerobics is booming business. *Reader's Digest* recently reported that "for an overwhelming majority of men, being muscular—with wide shoulders, well-developed arms and chest, and a narrow waist—is as tyrannical a standard for men as being slender is for women."[2] As a group, Americans spend roughly $300 million on plastic surgery every year and a whopping $20 billion on cosmetics.[3] A recent article asserted that "94 percent of men would like to change some aspect of their physical appearance."[4] The concern with, and pursuit of, beauty is alive and well.

A long history

Through the ages people have been aware of personal appearance. In Bible times Jezebel wore eye makeup, Samson realized his attraction to the opposite sex was because of his strength, Esther dabbed on perfume, and Absalom's prospective royal subjects were drawn to him largely because of his youthful, handsome features and spectacular head of hair.

In Elizabethan England women treated skin spots and freckles with components of mercury, sulfur, and turpentine.[5]

Until this century parents in China bound the feet of little girls in order to keep their walk delicate in appearance. One tribe in Kenya still adorns its daughters with tight metal necklaces in order to achieve graceful, elongated necks by the time the little girls become young women.

And we're still at it today! In this country men and women pay millions of dollars a year to publishers of *GQ, Vogue,* and other magazines in an attempt to get "help" for their own appearance. How did Oprah lose 80 pounds? What low-cal recipes do leading actresses use? What is the secret of one celebrity's "wrinkle-defying smile"? (She pretends to have a fishhook in each corner of her mouth!)[6] At the same time, readers are secretly and despondently comparing themselves to the beautiful models featured in these magazines.

Why?

After looking with disappointment into a mirror, what makes us arm ourselves with checkbook or credit card and set out on yet another foray through cosmetic counter aisles, clothing stores, and fashion magazines? Why this pursuit of beauty?

---

[1] Cathleen Rountree, *On Women Turning 50* (San Francisco: Harper San Francisco, 1996), p. 6.

[2] Shelley Levitt, "What Women Don't Know About Today's Men," *Reader's Digest*, October 1995, p. 63.

[3] Rountree, p. 6.

[4] Levitt, p. 63.

[5] Rosemounde of Mercia and Wolf Federweiss, eds., "Cosmetics," *The Compleat Anachronist* (Douglas, Alaska: 1991), p. 14.

[6] *Women's World,* Jan. 19, 1995, p. 43.

CHAPTER 9

THIN ENOUGH . . . FOR WHAT?

One group of language specialists have agreed that the six sweetest phrases in the English language are the following: "I love you." "Dinner is served." "All is forgiven." "Sleep until noon." "Keep the change." And . . . "You've lost weight!"
—L. M. Boyd

Let's look at several possible motivations for our pursuit of beauty. Perhaps someone important in our early lives modeled the pursuit of beauty.

I remember watching my beautiful grandma Maybelle saturate her face and hands with cream before bedtime and then slip on white cotton gloves to keep her creamed hands moist overnight. Grandma Josephine, whom I also adored, drank homemade garlic juice to keep herself beautiful from the inside out.

At 78 my own mother continues to be the most beautiful woman I know. My father once identified her real beauty secret, which he confided to me when we were alone.

"Your mother," he said, "is the most generous person I have ever known. Everybody loves her."

I guess they do, because last Mother's Day, although she has only two children—my younger brother and me—she received 16 Mother's Day cards. They came from the hairdresser, previous teaching colleagues, the Korean couple at the photo shop she patronizes, and the UPS man. My dad says he understands the attraction.

So early role models might have something to do with our pursuit of beauty.

Fashion mag intimidation

A second possible reason for our beauty pursuit might be the stigma our nineties culture attempts to place on individuals who don't embody its unrealistic physical standards. Just recently my hometown's newspaper carried an Associated Press article bearing the ruthless headline "Old-Crone Comic as Ugly as Ever."[1] What followed was a short piece on the aging comedienne Phyllis Diller. But then, I suppose Phyllis doesn't help her cause much by saying, "When I go to the beauty parlor, I always use the emergency entrance. Sometimes I just go for an estimate."[2]

On different occasions through the years friends have confided that when they take a hiatus from looking at fashion magazines, they begin to feel much more comfortable with how they look. But after a "fashion mag binge," they tend to become depressed with everything about their appearance.

A couple years ago *real, live* people wrote articles about the midlife passage of Barbie (the doll with unrealistic dimensions) turning 35.[3] In the past 35 years how many women, thinking they would grow up to look like Barbie in adulthood, have felt cheated by life when they grew up to look like real people instead? Because of this, those in the "appearance" business prey upon our insecurities by offering us hope for our physical shortcomings.

The title of one magazine article screamed, "Help! I Have No Eyebrows!"[4] Another article's lead-in assured the reader, "Now there's hope for veiny, bony hands—you can make them look younger and more supple with a little fat from your thigh." (Incidentally, for a mere $1,000 to $1,500.)[5]

Even political leaders are not immune from our culture's fashion-conscious scrutiny. Last year *Life* magazine posed this probing question: "Is President Clinton just retaining water?"[6] This preoccupation with physical appearance pervades our very language. A discount coupon for a beauty shop asked potential customers the question "Are you having a 'bad hair day'?"

Cultural stigma, then, might be a second reason for some who pursue beauty.

Thirty-nine and holding

A third reason some people so actively pursue beauty may be a fear that the aging process is stealthily stealing what youth contributed earlier. So many women are self-conscious about divulging their ages that fashion designer Christian Dior made this comment: "Women are most fascinating between the ages of 35 and 40 . . . [and since] few women ever pass 40, maximum fascination can continue indefinitely."[7]

Before we proceed any further, let me remind us all that aging is inevitable. The two best ways I know of to deal with this concern are these:

First, we can enjoy the wisdom we're gaining over a lifetime and just take the rest in stride. One jovial senior poet purportedly penned these lines in a letter to an understanding friend:

> "Just a line to say I'm living,
> that I'm not among the dead

Though I'm getting more forgetful
  and mixed up in the head . . .
I got used to my arthritis,
  to my dentures I'm resigned.
I can manage my bifocals,
  but I sure do miss my mind . . .
And I stand before the mailbox,
  with a face so very red
Instead of mailing you my letter,
  I had opened it instead."[8]

Second, instead of worrying about encroaching age, we can focus on God's ageless goodness to us. The writer of Ecclesiastes 5:20 did this when he wrote, "For he will not often consider the years of his life, because God keeps him occupied with the gladness of his heart" (NASB).

Shaky self-esteem

Another reason that goads people to pursue beauty is that they suffer from low self-esteem. Scott Peck states that "We all have this unrealistic sense of our unimportance, of our unloveliness and undesirability.[9] I suspect that most of us experience shaky self-esteem, for whatever reasons—negative childhood environment, unfavorable parental comparison between siblings, poor performance in school, rejection by someone of the opposite sex, having felt like a loner on occasion.

Beautiful enough . . . for what?

Perhaps the fifth and most basic reason for our pursuit of beauty lies within the results of a survey taken by *Life* magazine. In an article entitled "Do I Look Fat to You (or Is It All in My Head)?" researchers disclosed the findings of a 29-question survey about "our national obsession."[10]

They began their conclusion like this: "In our closets, hanging like old calendars, are the dresses and suits we wore a few winters ago, when we were 10 pounds thinner but still not thin enough. Thin enough for what?" the researchers asked before rendering their heartbreaking conclusion: "Thin enough to be loved."[11]

Might this conclusion also be an answer to the question of why so many pursue beauty? Although many of us might not care to admit it, is it not perhaps about being beautiful enough someday . . . to be loved?

But by whom? By our friends? By someone we hope to attract? By ourselves? By God, even?

Although we've briefly explored five possible motivations for the pursuit of beauty, do we really know what we are after? What is true beauty, anyway?

[1] Grants Pass *Daily Courier*, Oct. 10, 1994, p. 12.

[2] Phyllis Diller, as quoted in *Age Before Beauty* (White Plains, N.Y.: Peter Pauper Press, Inc.), 1991.

[3] *Women's World*, Jan. 10, 1995, p. 23. Also *Working Woman*, November 1994, p. 12.

[4] "Help! I Have No Eyebrows!" *Women's World*, Jan. 31, 1994, p. 23.

[5] Sherri Dalphonse, "Reversing Hands of Time," *The Washingtonian*, November 1994, p. 111.

[6] Lisa Grunwald, "Do I Look Fat to You (or Is It All in My Head)?" *Life*, February 1995, p. 66.

[7] As quoted in *The Reader's Digest Treasury of Modern Quotations* (New York: Reader's Digest, 1975), p. 395.

[8] Tal D. Bonham and Jack Gulledge, *The Treasury of Clean Senior Adult Jokes* (Nashville: Broadman Press, 1989), pp. 93, 94.

[9] M. Scott Peck, *Further Along the Road Less Traveled* (New York: Simon and Schuster, 1993), p. 98.

[10] Grunwald, p. 58.

[11] *Ibid.*

CHAPTER 10

EASY STEP 1: GIVE GOD A CALL

Groanings which cannot be uttered are often prayers which cannot be refused.
—Charles H. Spurgeon

Helplessness united with faith produces prayer.
—O. Hallesby

Although he lived a long time ago and was never known by the title International Expert on Beauty, that is exactly what the apostle Paul was. Except for Jesus Himself, no other Bible character has so much to say about the Magnificent Makeover. And certainly no one else has explained it quite as thoroughly as Paul did when he wrote his Epistles to the Galatians and Romans.

Since Paul outlined the simple steps of the Magnificent Makeover some 2,000 years ago, lesser beauty "experts" have revised Paul's makeover plan into such a lengthy, complicated, laborious process that understanding it is sometimes a remote possibility. Yet other "experts" have simplified Paul's description of the makeover so much that some of the essential phases have not only been considered less important, but often have been left out completely.

Hoping to become a "madeover" beauty by following either of these beauty program revisions is futile. Someone who attempts to become beautiful by following the regimen of the more complicated program revision will often end up confused, discouraged, and having to make continual, self-conscious checks in her spiritual mirror. Some who follow this particular program are also known to check on—and assess—the beauty progress of those around them, as well.

And a person who follows the simplified version of the Magnificent Makeover usually risks becoming flabby and careless about beauty maintenance—even to the point of encouraging this lack of fitness in others.

Only by faithfully following the easy steps introduced so clearly by Christ and explained so well by Paul does one become the astonishing beauty God intended her to be. What are these easy steps? I understand

and remember them best by using the acronym GROW. In this chapter and the rest of this section we will explore what each of the letters in GROW stands for—and how each of these phases contributes to the Magnificent Makeover.

G stands for "Give God a call." Paul states that "whosoever shall call upon the name of the Lord shall be saved" (Rom. 10:13).

Calling for help

We most often call upon someone when we recognize our need for help in some matter. Calling someone for help brings back memories of midyear, fourth grade. No one could have prepared me for the pain of post-tonsillectomy swallowing.

Sometime during that first night back home from the hospital, I awoke from a fitful sleep—and swallowed! With raw pain overwhelming me, and with the collected mucus in my sinuses making inhalation through my nostrils impossible, I knew I was going to die. In spite of my fiery throat, I made a desperate attempt to call for help. All that came from my voice box was a raspy, helpless groan.

But my father heard. I knew he would. Suddenly he was there by my side with his big, warm hand over mine. I wanted so much to tell him to get Mother and Wally, my brother, and Skippy, the Boston terrier, so I could tell them all goodbye. I tried to tell him, but somehow it all got mixed up, and what came out was the croaking plea "Daddy, put your arms around me."

In an instant he was scooping me up in his strong arms and telling me how much he was hurting along with me. Somehow, with him holding me like that, it didn't matter so much that I tell him anything else.

The next thing I knew the morning sun was slicing through the crack in my curtains, and I was feeling better already.

An act of faith

Giving God a call is an act of faith. "The just shall live by faith," Paul tells us (Rom. 1:17). Giving God a call also means we turn our sins over to Him and enlist Him as the senior partner in our making the necessary changes to avoid those sins in the future. And how free God is with forgiveness! "If we confess our sins, he is faithful and just to forgive us our sins, and to cleanse us from all unrighteousness" (1 John 1:9).

"The voice of sin may be loud," said D. L. Moody, "but the voice of forgiveness is louder."[1]

Ellen White wrote that "tears of the penitent are only the raindrops that precede the sunshine of holiness."[2]

Best of all, God has promised to answer when we call on Him. "Then shalt thou call, and the Lord shall answer; thou shalt cry, and he shall say, Here I am" (Isa. 58:9).

The first phase of the Magnificent Makeover is to give God that call, not just once, but every time we feel our need of Him. And . . . we are always in need of Him.

[1] Dwight L. Moody, in Steven Mosley, *There I Go Again* (Dallas: Word Publishing, 1991), p. 29.

[2] E. G. White, *The Desire of Ages* (Mountain View, Calif.: Pacific Press Pub. Assn., 1898), p. 300.

CHAPTER 11

EASY STEP 2:
RECEIVE HIS GIFTS

Waves pound the bow
of this fragile frigate
on a cold, sunshiny day.
Through salt spray
they flash on impact—
millisecond rainbows
of grace.
—Carolyn Rathbun

When we give God a call for help, He stands ready to rain down upon us the abundance of heaven. Step 2 of the Magnificent Makeover, represented by R in the acronym GROW, calls upon us to "Receive God's gifts of grace."

Paul says that although death reigned because of one man, Adam, we can now "reign in life" through another Man, Jesus Christ (Rom. 5:17, NASB). All we have to do for this fact to be accomplished in our lives is to *"receive the abundance of grace."*

The concept of grace, often defined as "unmerited favor," is so mind-boggling that I don't hope to be able to understand it fully this side of heaven. In the meantime, however, those glimpses—those neon sign flashes of understanding—into the riches of God's grace keep coming. For me, those flashes occur quietly in the unrolling events in my daily life, such as that afternoon when for one brief moment I was heralded as a national hero.

Firestorm

In late August 1987 a firestorm, caused when a series of lightning-induced forest fires in the Sierra Nevadas converged, forced our mountain community to be evacuated. For four days, while we caught glimpses of our endangered community on nationally televised newscasts at the home of friends who had taken us in, I felt so unworthy of the life-threatening risks firefighters from around the country were taking to save my home. Calling the local Red Cross and county fairgrounds evacuation centers, I asked if I could assist in any way.

"One more person in here would make things tighter than they already are," a harried-sounding official told me.

I felt useless and helpless. Returning home after our brief exile, we residents of Twain Harte felt gratitude and affection for the men and women who had kept our homes from being reduced to mounds of charred rubble. They became the instant heroes of Tuolumne County. "Firefighters, We Love You" signs went up along the highway and roads.

A couple days later, after schools reopened, my principal sent me on an errand to Modesto after classes. As I fell in behind a 10-engine convoy of firefighters returning from another hot spot, my heart once again filled with unspeakable gratitude for these exhausted, soot-weary warriors who had risked so much for me.

Trailing heroes

Although I stayed a few respectful car lengths back, when the highway widened into four lanes I crept past the escort car and drew abreast of the last fire engine. The driver, happening to glance down, smiled. A little embarrassed, but emboldened, I drew alongside the second engine, and the third, and then the fourth. The gold insignia on the door read "Fire Department, Moraga, California." What a tired-looking crew! Yet I felt a measure of excitement at being so close to nationally televised heroes.

I was just about to pull even with the fifth engine when my lane narrowed abruptly. I'd been paying so much attention to my heroes and their equipment that I had not been noticing the road signs. The driver of the truck from Moraga noticed my predicament and hit his brakes, motioning me to pull in ahead of him.

Suddenly I became uneasy; had I just done something illegal? After all, hadn't I just sort of intercepted the line of an officially escorted convoy?

"Road Construction Ahead. Prepare to Stop!" a sign warned. The next thing I knew, we—the convoy and I—were being flagged to the shoulder of the road. *Oh, brother!* A sinking sensation in my stomach suggested I was somewhere I wasn't supposed to be.

Guilt

To add to my growing consternation, a badged official from the fire marshal's escort vehicle at the front of the line appeared, walking down the line of trucks—in my direction. With the air-conditioner off now, the outside temperature around $96°F$, and the windows still rolled tight under a hot afternoon sun, my eyeglasses started slowly slipping toward the end of my perspiring nose. Avoiding eye contact with the ever-approaching fire marshal, I was momentarily distracted by loud voices. Suddenly, from out of nowhere, a thundering explosion roared across the top of my vehicle, rocking it violently. I screamed and jerked my head around. Through foamy cascades running down my window, I was able to distinguish three firefighters wrestling with a big fire hose whose gushing nozzle they quickly pointed away from my car and toward a field on the other side of a barbed-wire fence.

That's it! I thought. *I've just been zapped with the Firefighters' Seal of Disapproval, and it's only going to get worse.*

Sure enough. In my rearview mirror I could see two of "them" striding toward my car. My imagination ran wild and for an instant I pictured myself before a judge, trying to explain why I'd broken into an officially escorted firefighting convoy on its way to take care of urgent business. *I mustn't roll down my window even an inch,* I decided, *or they'll be able to slip through the subpoena.* I could just see the writing on the courtroom wall: *Firefighters of America vs. Rathbun.*

An insistent knocking on the car window brought this horrifying reverie to an abrupt halt.

Grace

"Ma'am," called a voice through my tightly closed window, "we had an accident with our fire hose."

"Yeah," called a second man loudly, "we didn't mean to get your car all wet—although it's really clean now."

"Here," offered the first, still at high volume, "have something to drink—on us."

Returning somewhat to my normal senses, I began to realize that these men hadn't approached to serve me court orders. Managing to roll down the window a few inches, I extended my hands for a couple of the drinks, but was still unable to speak.

"You sure you're all right, ma'am?" the fireman asked. "Now, once again, your car appears to be fine, so don't worry."

Dumbly, I nodded. The men exchanged an uneasy glance, then in the uncertain silence, and using mostly backward steps, they cautiously withdrew from my presence. I spent the next half hour taking long drafts of cold soda and finishing my English paper corrections while I waited. Sounds of laughter from a group of firefighters leaning against the front of the Moraga truck drifted through the car window. Glancing at them in the rearview mirror, I mused, *Maybe these are some of the very ones who saved our home. Because of them we will have a roof over our heads tonight.* I remembered my husband's highly complicated Nikon camera behind the car seat. *I'll bet he'd like to have a picture of that engine. But it might be too nervy of me to ask . . .*

Hesitantly, I eased out of the car, wrestling with the camera case. Walking back toward the fire engine, I timidly said, "Excuse me . . . thanks for the drinks . . . uh, would you mind terribly if I took a picture of your truck? Uh, you can just stay there, if you like." Then I couldn't hold it in any longer.

"You guys," I choked out, surprised at my emotion, "you guys—or some just like you—saved our house this week. We're really, really grateful." Then I started fumbling with the camera adjustments and blinking back tears. The fireman who'd given me the sodas approached.

And more grace

"If we saved your house, ma'am, that makes us feel real good. By the way, I think I know how to work these things," he said, taking the camera from me. "Now you go 'long over there and get in that picture too."

Oh! I thought. *My little pink schoolteacher dress is so wrinkled!* And now I suddenly regretted not having taken the time to put in my contact lenses that morning! But I walked over to the group. One fireman put a kind arm about my shoulders, two others leaned in, and we all said, "Cheese."

At that moment, a line of what must have been 60 vehicles from the other end of the road construction site began driving by. Seeing the fire engine convoy and the firefighters, the drivers and their occupants went wild, honking, shouting, waving.

Thank yous and God bless yous and We love yous filled the air. From all around me came the hearty but modest replies: "We're happy to do it!" "You're welcome!" "You bet!" The fireman who had taken the picture handed me back the camera.

"Hey, you're all national heroes, you know!" one burly driver called jubilantly to them, or rather called to us. For the photographer-fireman, with a twinkle in his eye, had just nodded to me, indicating *I* should wave back at the oncoming traffic as well.

So there in the middle of that circle of heroes, awash in cacophonous waves of gratitude and love, I too stood and waved and received unmerited praise—a neon flash of unmerited, amazing grace. I, the unworthy one, unworthy of those refreshing drinks; unworthy of inclusion in a portrait of heroes; unworthy of those lives risked for my house—the house of a stranger. I who had wanted to do something—anything—at the evacuation centers to be deserving. But I who in the end did nothing—nothing but cause my heroes even extra trouble.

Double exposure!

What a story I had to tell my husband that night! And what a picture I had to show!

And what a picture God holds in His hand of you and me when we receive His grace, standing right there next to our Hero, His Son. God looks at that picture, and the resemblance between us and His holy Son is uncanny. Do you have any doubt about your beauty when God looks at His picture?

"How beautiful you are, . . . how beautiful you are! . . . there is no blemish in you" (S. of Sol. 4:1-7, NASB). Receive God's amazing grace. Amazing because it's there simply for the taking. And God's gift-giving doesn't stop with just grace. The extravagant Gift-giver sends along two other unspeakable gifts: Christ's righteousness (to cover our sinfulness) and the presence of the Holy Spirit (to help us live a beautiful life).

CHAPTER 12

CONGRATULATIONS!

Worship the Lord in the beauty of holiness.
—Psalm 29:2

Just today I pulled a thick "Official Notice" envelope out of my mailbox. Here is what the largest, boldface type shouted from the page:

YOU'VE HIT THE BIG ONE, CAROLYN RATHBUN— YOU'VE WON THE FIRST ELEVEN MILLION DOLLAR PRIZE IN OUR HISTORY!

This jarring announcement was prefaced by an introductory clause (in small print): "If you have and return the big winning entry, we'll say . . ." Another insert informed me that "prize officials have just identified you as a grand prize candidate—one step away from a giant cash award!"

What a coincidence! Those officials identified me as a grand prize candidate last year, too—*and* the year before that! Wow! Lucky me! The only problem is that my candidacy has remained "just one step away from a fortune most people only dream about." I've never yet been selected as the grand prize winner—not even once.

A long time ago I stopped getting excited about notices such as this one. Too many odds are against *this* subscriber having much of a chance at winning the sweepstakes. Besides, those semifinalist "winner" notices are usually too good to be true.

But what would you think if you received an "Official Notice" in the mail that stated the following:

Congratulations! You are a HOLY person! Because of your unique status, escrow is currently closing on the soon-to-be-yours 500-acre ranch estate, as well as on your new suburban mansion. In addition, the riches of the universe are now at your disposal. No strings attached!

Far-fetched? Not really. For you, special lady, became not only beautiful, but also holy, after completing the first two steps of the Magnificent Makeover: giving God a call and receiving His grace. You were "justified as a gift by His grace through the redemption which is in Christ Jesus" (Rom. 3:24, NASB). Without your even having to subscribe to a magazine, Heaven declared you a grand prize winner, and *you won the sweepstakes!* You became justified before the throne of grace.

Being justified means two things. First, it denotes "pardon, remission, and nonimputation of all sins, reconciliation to God, and the end of his enmity and wrath" toward breakers of His "holy law" (Acts 13:39; Rom. 4:6, 7; 2 Cor. 5:19; Rom. 5:9).[1] Second, being justified means being in the position of a righteous person with "a title to all the blessings promised to the just. . . ."[2] Paul tells us that by justification we are adopted into God's family as children and heirs (Rom. 8:14; Gal. 4:4, 5). In fact, the entire theme of Romans is God offering His gift of righteousness to anyone who puts faith in Christ (Rom. 1:16, 17).

"Wait a minute!" you say. "We've been discussing beauty. What does beauty have to do with holiness? Aren't you bending logic here?"

The beauty of holiness

I don't think so. The Bible itself relates beauty to holiness. Both Psalm 29:2 and Psalm 96:9 call us to "worship the Lord in the beauty of holiness."

A strange and astonishing story about the beauty of holiness appears in 2 Chronicles 20. Judah, under the reign of King Jehoshaphat, suffered an overwhelming military threat from the combined forces of the Moabites, the Ammonites, and the inhabitants of the area of Mount Seir. After King Jehoshaphat led his people in a fast and prayer vigil, God sent a message through a priest, giving the king permission to march into battle.

Early the next morning Jehoshophat appointed a choir to march before the army. He instructed them not to sing "Onward, Christian Soldiers," but rather to praise the "beauty of holiness" (2 Chron. 20:21). As the choir marched forth, singing and praising the beauty of holiness, God set ambushments against the enemy. When Jehoshaphat's infantry arrived, they found not one enemy foot soldier left alive. The Hebrew army had nothing to do for the next three days except cart away the spoils of a battle God had fought for them.

The legendary Helen of Troy was reputedly so beautiful she became known as the "face that launched a thousand ships." Homer's legend tells how two great Greek city-states fought over her—for a decade. But Helen's beauty pales in comparison to this "beauty of holiness" that in a few hours' time is capable of conquering the military machinery and fighting forces of three powerful nations!

What is holiness?

The apostle Paul urges us to be "partakers of his holiness" (Heb. 12:10). God Himself calls us to this beauty through His words to the children of Israel: "Ye shall be holy; for I am holy" (Lev. 11:44).

But what *is* holiness? Holiness is a concept not easily understood, for it is the very foundation of God's personhood. "Holy, holy, holy is the Lord of hosts" (Isa. 6:3). Characteristics of holiness can be found throughout the Old Testament. These include awesomeness (Gen. 28:17), divine sacredness (Ex. 3:5), separateness (Hosea 11:9), purity and moral perfection (Hab. 1:13), and consecration (Lev. 11:44). And, of course, all these facets of holiness are seen throughout the New Testament in the life and witness of Jesus Christ.[3]

Both in the Old Testament (particularly Leviticus) and the New Testament (1 Peter 1:16), writers stress the importance of our walking in holiness on an everyday basis.

How you "got" holy

You became beautiful and holy by completing the first two steps Paul so beautifully explains in Romans and Galatians. In going through step 1 of the Magnificent Makeover, giving God a call, you unconditionally opened your spirit to the *whatevers*, the *wherevers*, and the *whoevers* in heaven's personalized makeover program for you. You admitted you could not go it alone, that you have no real or lasting beauty outside of His love.

You received God's gifts when you, with His help, completed step 2 of the Magnificent Makeover. You put down your umbrella (or shield) and let God rain His grace upon you. His grace overwhelmed you. His righteousness washed you inside and out—and covered you. His constant forgiveness encouraged and softened you. And His power fortified you to be strong in the ways His loving Spirit leads you. "That power is Christ. His grace alone can quicken the lifeless faculties of the soul, and attract it to God, to holiness."[4]

At the end of step 2, because of your belief, your faith, God's Spirit separated you from the commonplace. He consecrated you. And you, in turn, devoted yourself to His will.

Congratulations! You won the sweepstakes. You have been declared a holy person, and the riches of heaven are yours. No strings attached—for *you*, anyway. The only strings in this arrangement bound Christ to the cross. Because of Him, you are a walking picture of the beauty of holiness, a ravishing beauty.

Experts have long agreed that a major benefit of working toward a stress-reduced lifestyle is more peace of mind. Paul, in Romans 5:1, clearly states the benefit resulting from a person's completion of Step 2: "Therefore being justified by faith, we have peace with God through our Lord Jesus Christ."

How does one "maintain" the makeover?

As a wedding anniversary gift for her husband, a friend of mine once paid big bucks for a makeover, and then posed for a variety of photography studio shots. Three weeks later, after she'd chosen from the photographer's proofs, she compiled for her spouse a lush little photograph album containing only portraits of herself. She offered to let me look through the album before she giftwrapped it.

As I looked enviously through the absolutely smashing pictures, she commented with satisfaction, "I think these pictures make me look as good as possible."

As good as possible? No way! Thanks to the makeover, the studio lighting, and the glamorous clothing the studio had furnished, let me tell you that my friend looked *better* than possible!

As I handed the album back to her, she opened to the shot of herself in a turquoise sundress and said wistfully, "Wish I could look this way all the time. After the makeover I looked truly wonderful—for about six hours—and then it all began wearing off. I never learned how to maintain a makeover."

God assumed responsibility for making us over in steps 1 and 2 of the Magnificent Makeover. We now have the option of working with Him to maintain that holiness that has become ours. It is a matter of choice. "Therefore, having these promises, beloved, let us cleanse ourselves from all defilement of flesh and spirit, perfecting holiness in the fear of God" (2 Cor. 17).

Steps 1 and 2 give us the *initial* makeover, the jump-start. Step 3 describes the *progressive,* or *practical,* part of this makeover.

---

[1] Walter A. Elwell, ed., "Justification," *Evangelical Dictionary of Theology* (Grand Rapids: Baker Book House, 1984), p. 594.

[2] *Ibid.,* p. 514.

[3] *Synonyms of the New Testament,* in the *New American Standard Bible,* New Open Bible Study Edition (Nashville: Thomas Nelson Publishers, 1990), p. 1,445.

[4] Ellen G. White, *Steps to Christ* (Mountain View, Calif.: Pacific Press Pub. Assn., 1956), p. 18.

CHAPTER 13

(NOT SO) EASY STEP 3: OBEY HIS PROMPTINGS

As you therefore have received Christ Jesus the Lord [justification], *so walk in Him* [sanctification].
—*Colossians 2:6, NASB*

If ye be willing and obedient, ye shall eat the good of the land.
—*Isaiah 1:19*

The (not so) easy Step 3 of the Magnificent Makeover toward the beauty of holiness has to do with one of God's gifts to us—the indwelling of the Holy Spirit. The letter O in the acronym GROW stands for "Obey the loving promptings of His Spirit."

In describing a curate's discussion with his parishioners, George MacDonald wrote that the curate explained "that faith and obedience are one and the same spirit: what in the heart we call faith, in the will we call obedience."[1] Ah, but obedience, disciplining the will, is where the rubber meets the road!

Obedience is our response to His gifts to us. It is a physical demonstration to God that we love Him. "If you love me, you will obey what I command" (John 14:15, NIV). W. Bingham Hunter states that "if we obey, we grow to know the mind of God and we will begin to pray according to His will. Such prayers are answered."[2] Obedience through the strength of His Spirit brings us close to God. The Spirit never moves without loving purpose. But those moments, especially when we don't understand the purpose behind divine urgings, may be the most important decision moments of our lives.

Sailing with the wind

About three summers ago some of my high school students talked me into going with them for a weeklong sailing course as a sailing cadet on the mission ship *Canvasback*. In one lecture aboard the vessel, the captain explained that in light winds of three to five knots, we needed only a drifter, or foresail.

"However," said the captain, "when the first gust of a stronger wind comes up, stretching your drifter sail, that's the signal to change your sails. Drop the drifter, put up the heavier mainsail, and get on course immediately." Then he added, "Stay on course!"

In John 3:8 Jesus explains to Nicodemus that the Holy Spirit is like a wind. "The wind blows where it chooses, and you hear the sound of it, but you do not know where it comes from or where it goes. So it is with everyone who is born of the Spirit" (NRSV).

Troubled visitor

One Friday afternoon Mariya, a student of mine, knocked at the door. Mariya's family were refugees from a neighboring African nation. In addition to a sense of displacement, she was grappling with the recent loss of her mother, who had been killed while riding in the back of a pickup truck, the local mode of public transportation. Mariya was also grappling with the reality of a new stepmother, whose side of the family hated Mariya.

With a dozen presundown tasks to finish in the next hour and a half, the last thing I felt like doing was sitting down for small talk. I knew, though, that in this culture small talk always precedes the real reason for a visit.

The wind of the Spirit blew its first gentle puff into my drifter sail.

Sensing my stress, Mariya soon said, "Madamu, you must be busy; I will leave now and come back another time."

It is customary in that part of Africa for a host to accompany a visitor at least part of the way home, since the guest has made a great effort to come to one's house on foot. But Mariya said, "You don't have to accompany me today. Return to your work."

The wind was now stretching my drifter sail.

But I didn't want to take the time to make any course changes, or get on a different course just then. After all, Mariya *had* released me from the obligation of accompanying her.

The wind distorted my drifter sail to the point of discomfort.

I knew I had not made her comfortable enough to state the real reason for her visit. When she stood to leave, I stood up as well.

But instead of letting me stop at the front door, the wind blew me out after her.

As we walked up the dirt road, I asked, "Mariya, what is it?"

"I'm afraid," she said, and then seemed unable to say any more.

While I waited for her to continue, a word from a recent language lesson popped into my mind. But it was a word that was taboo, at least to speak in public. Then, unexpectedly, I said, *"Abazimu,"* a word that means "spirits of the dead."

Mariya looked at me in shock while I stared back at her in disbelief.

"What did you say?" she gasped.

With one final blast, the wind dropped the drifter sail and pulled the mainsail into place.

I repeated the word, in an intentional whisper this time, still not understanding why I was saying it.

Mariya bit her lip, looked off into the distance, and then back at me. Her eyes held terror.

How did you know?

"Madamu, how did you know?" Leading me to the back veranda of a vacant mission house, my student poured out the story of how her hostile stepgrandmother was insisting on Mariya's presence at a mud-hut séance in order to receive an important message from the spirits of deceased ancestors.

"How can I do this thing?" Mariya asked. "I'm a Christian now. But if I don't, I will alienate my family." She continued, "And my stepgrandmother has warned me that if I don't meet with the spirits to receive their message, a curse will be placed on me. I will never live long enough to bear children—or even get married."

Looking at me in desperation, Mariya pleaded, "Madamu, tell me what to do."

"Well," I sputtered, my mind in a whirl, "you need to pray and study the Bible and have faith that God will show you what to do."

She looked at me with frightened eyes and asked, "How do you get faith like that? I'm not sure I really know how to pray. I'm a new Christian—I don't know how to study the Bible." She paused and then quietly pleaded, "Teach me."

Setting a new course

I drew a deep breath before asking, "When shall we start?"

Because of the heavy Belgian educational system that our school followed, the only mutually possible time was 5:00 in the morning. Mariya suggested that since we had no electricity that time of day (the school had it only between 6:30 and 9:30 at night), we meet outside somewhere. That way we would bother neither the other girls in the dormitory nor my family. She suggested a flat rocky outcropping near the eucalyptus forest not far from the girls' dorm.

False start

For every current of divine wind, there is a countercurrent, because the adversary would have us not follow the loving prompting of the Holy Spirit. Do you know how much I hate getting up at 4:45 in the morning? I'm not very crazy about going outside in the dark by myself, either.

Nevertheless, the next Tuesday morning found me stepping into the predawn blackness at 4:50. After fearfully walking some 50 paces up the road, I heard what sounded like a large animal bearing down on me from behind. My heart felt as though it had stopped beating. I could do nothing but turn around and face the sound of racing paws on the dry, sandy road.

As I heard the creature gulp air and leap, I instinctively raised a knee and caught the animal square in the chest and heard it go sprawling. The thinly flickering beam of my flashlight revealed Pookie, the neighbors' dim-witted dog, cowering at my feet. Catching my breath, I whispered a hoarse "Go home!" and left it whimpering in the road while I continued toward the dark eucalyptus forest.

Mariya and I met on Tuesday and Thursday that week. The next week she asked if she could bring Antoinette. The following week Antoinette invited Helena. The week after that Helena brought Dorcas and Damaris. Our little group continued to grow. Twice a week we met, by flashlight and kerosene lantern—and then by dawn's faint rays. Sometimes we huddled under a canopy of umbrellas, because these girls didn't allow heavy fog or mild rainstorms to quench the thirst they had for knowledge about God.

Answered prayers

We studied about faith and prayer and repentance and the Second Coming. As we all grew in faith and in spiritual accountability to the Lord and to each other, I grew to love so much my precious younger sisters in Jesus.

At the end of the first school year, Mariya returned home. There, backed by continuing prayers from the rest of the group and by her own walk of faith, she politely but firmly confronted her stepgrandmother. Courageously Mariya made it clear that she would not meet for that séance—ever. The grandmother became livid but, astonishingly, put no more pressure on Mariya to contact the spirits. This was, by far, the most exciting answered prayer that first year.

Compounded interest

The following school year one of the older girls asked if my feelings would be hurt should she stop coming to the early morning group. She quickly added, "Some of the younger girls in the dorm want to learn to study and pray too. But they're afraid to come out in the dark so early. I think God wants me to start a group for them later in the morning."

The wind was prompting her to change her sails as well.

At the end of the second school year two of the older girls graduated. Antoinette started a nursing course at an Adventist hospital in the eastern part of the country. Helena went up north to begin her first year as a primary school teacher.

Antoinette started a prayer group for her peers in nursing school and Helena began one with her young students. Now three groups exchanged letters of praise and shared requests and held each other up in prayer. *And the wind continued to blow.*

The wind has its reasons

When our family left Africa forever two and a half years after the start of the first prayer group, I thought my heart would break at that last early-morning gathering. But we solemnly promised each other and the Lord that no matter what happened to us in life, we would put Jesus first and regroup someday under the tree of life.

Most of the girls continued to write me after our return to the States—always with news of conversions, answered prayers, and continued growth in Jesus. Twelve years after I left Africa, Mariya wrote that she was living with her doctoral candidate husband and two small children. She was still exulting in the superiority of faith and prayer over the powers of darkness.

For the past two years, however, I have received no letters from Mariya or from any of the other prayer group girls whom I grew to love so much there on those flat rocks near the eucalyptus forest on a hillside . . . in Rwanda. Few of them, if any, are still alive.

The wind of the Spirit always moves with purpose.

And what amazing feats God has accomplished through individuals who chose to live in holy obedience to the loving promptings of His Spirit.

Naaman saved his skin.

Esther saved a nation.

Noah saved a civilization.

And Jesus saved a universe.

---

[1] George MacDonald, in *Knowing the Heart of God* (Minneapolis: Bethany House Pubs., 1990), p. 35.

[2] W. Bingham Hunter, *The God Who Hears* (Downers Grove, Ill.: InterVarsity Press, 1986), p. 148.

CHAPTER 14

EASY STEP 4:
WATCH THE BEAUTY GROW!

I called—He came;
He gave—I took;
With Spirit's help,
My sins forsook.
The Holy Gardener,
At my call,
Made me a beauty . . .
After all!
    —Carolyn Rathbun

A seed growing secretly"[1] is how C. S. Lewis described the growth of holiness. The final phase of the Magnificent Makeover process is represented by W in the acronym GROW: Watch the beauty grow!

As we follow the Spirit's promptings in our daily interactions—at home, at work, in the supermarket, at the gas station—a beautiful garden of holiness is springing up in our lives.

What grows in that garden is described by Paul in Galatians 5:22 and 23 as the "fruit of the Spirit": love, joy, peace, patience, gentleness, goodness, faith, meekness, and self-control.

These fruits are testimony to the fact that the progressive, practical aspects of the Magnificent Makeover are in place and that you, the "makeoveree," are continuing your journey more deeply into the beauty of holiness through a process known as sanctification, the process that qualifies one as a citizen fit for the heavenly kingdom.

For not with swords, loud clashing,
Nor roll of stirring drums,
With deeds of love and mercy,
The heavenly kingdom comes.[2]

Sanctification, a holy life, is both a process and a result. This means that not only is your initial makeover being continually enhanced, but also you are now daily walking through life as a woman who is confident in the beauty the Master Makeup Artist has given you.

I know how old you are!

Furthermore, the beautiful fruits of holiness in your life—if you haven't already noticed—attract others. Sometimes others see beauty in us that we didn't even know was there—like little Cassie saw in me. She approached me the second month of school.

"You're the new teacher, aren't you?" she greeted me one morning.

"Yes, I am."

"Well, I know how old you are!" she teased in a singsong voice.

I wasn't too surprised. Not only have I never disguised my age, but I had just recently told my junior high students that I'd be turning 50 within the month. I assumed Cassie had overheard, yet I decided to play along with her anyway.

"How old am I?" I asked.

Speaking matter-of-factly, with perfect confidence, she announced, "You're 17!"

"Oh, sweetheart!" I exclaimed, dropping to my knees and hugging her. "How did you know?"

"Well-l-l-l," she said as only a 7-year-old can, "I've been watching you. And—well-l-l-l—I just figured it out!" she proudly explained.

For the sake of integrity, I set the record straight, although I could tell that for Cassie the number 50 was an *infinite* number as far as she was concerned. And as far as God is concerned, *infinitely* beautiful is how we look to Him when we choose to experience His Magnificent Makeover in the shadow of the cross.

Three-part miracle with no bad hair days

The Magnificent Makeover, our growth into holiness, is a three-part miracle.

First, it's a miracle that the holy God can see any beauty in us at all.

Second, it's a miracle that He can open our eyes to see the beauty He's placed in what many of us have previously seen as our very ugly selves.

And finally, it's a miracle that when we recognize our own value, we almost automatically begin looking for the beauty in one another and nurturing others' growth as well.

Conscious of her beauty in the Lord, a woman doesn't have to worry about bad hair days ever again. She has only to recall that the very hairs of her head are numbered.

Remember that question (prompted by the *Life* magazine survey on dieting) that asked if one's pursuit of beauty is based on the hope of someday being beautiful enough to be loved? Well, at Calvary God showed us, beyond the shadow of a doubt, that we are beautiful, set apart from the commonplace, and valued precisely *because we are already loved.*

The invitation
God invites us to G-R-O-W daily in Him.

G: Give God those calls for help: Heavenly Father, put Your arms around me!

R: Receive God's amazing gifts: His grace, His righteousness, and His Holy Spirit.

O: Obey the loving promptings of His Spirit.

W: Watch the beauty grow—not only yours, but also the beauty of those whose lives your life touches.[3]

---

[1] C. S. Lewis, in *The Quotable Lewis,* eds. Wayne Martindale and Jerry Root (Wheaton, Ill.: Tyndale House Pubs., Inc., 1989), p. 303.

[2] Ernest W. Shurtleff, "Lead On, O King Eternal," *The Seventh-day Adventist Hymnal,* No. 619.

[3] W. F. Arndt, F. W. Gingrich, F. W. Danker, *A Greek-English Lexicon of the New Testament,* p. 9, in the *New American Standard Bible* New Open Bible Study Edition, p. 1,445.

CHAPTER 15

PETITION FOR BEAUTY

Holy Father,
Thank You that no matter where we've been in the past,
You continuously draw us back
    Into the garden of holiness, where
You take such incredible delight
    in making us over into Your image.

Some of us may be feeling unlovely,
    perhaps even unlovable.
Please—just now—
    reassure each one how very beautiful she is to You.

Lord, it is You who put into our hearts this yearning after beauty.
Put into our hearts as well the desire and strength
    for continued growth into the beauty of Your holiness.

We praise You.
We love You.
We pray these things in the name of Jesus Christ,
    Lord of all beauty.
            Amen.

Part Three

PORTRAIT OF A BEAUTIFUL WOMAN

CHAPTER 16

SHE LOOKS LIKE AN ARTIST: CHOOSING THE RIGHT COLORS

*One reassuring thing about modern art
is that things can't be as bad as they are painted.*
—M. Walthall Jackson

Trapped in summer school late one July, Cher, a nursing student, and I, an English major, were privately marveling (in a negative way) at some of the paintings brought back to the dormitory by two art majors. Looking at the random brushstrokes, we cast knowing glances at one another that meant "Yeah, right—we could do that."

In fact, modern art became such an inside joke with us that we decided late one night during a homework burnout crisis to put on an underground art show. The next evening, with colorful fingerpaints and four shades of Play-Doh purchased from the college market, with torn stockings and bent clothes hangers, Cher and I threw together about 25 pieces of "art"—each of which we named, of course.

At least two of the grotesque clay sculptures, among the hodgepodge we'd created, bore the pseudonyms of former boyfriends. And a few of our paintings alluded to certain faculty members from whom we'd gotten less than our favorite grade.

Underground art show

Next we clandestinely circulated "by invitation only" announcements inviting a few select friends to attend the "Ultimate Art Show." When we attempted to set up the exhibits on the afternoon preceding the show, we found our room was much too small. So we asked a couple friends if we could move our underground "happening" into their apartment at the end of the hall.

Soon we had our pseudocreations set up in the various apartment rooms—er, galleries. From the ceilings they hung, and from the walls and the venetian blinds and even from the light fixtures. The sculptures we carefully arranged along the desktops, windowsills, and across the beds, each piece placed carefully beside its identifying—or incriminating—title card. A punch bowl filled with M&Ms would provide the refreshments for this uptown event.

Party crashers

Unfortunately, the modest sign we had posted on our own door, with the arrow pointing to the art show's relocation, brought in more than our intended guests. In the midst of the hilarity with our friends over the phony art, about 15 elementary school teachers, returning from their summer school night class, burst excitedly through the door. It seems they were desperate for new classroom art ideas, because as they poured into our "galleries," they dropped their textbooks, opened their notebooks, and went right to work.

Cher and I anxiously stared at each other as these teachers moved with great interest from one piece of "art" to the next. Some of them made rough sketches of what we'd done, others asked about the materials used, and a couple of the more thoughtful ones inquired as to the meaning of our work.

Our bemused friends were watching my roommate and me doing a lot of fast talking when in walked one of the resident assistants, whose "likeness" (complete with chin wart) we had unfortunately captured in a lump of clay. I don't remember if it was Cher or I who quietly managed to drop-kick the potentially offending lump of Play-Doh under a bed before this latest unexpected visitor spotted it. I do remember, however, that the last half hour of the "Ultimate Art Show" came very close to turning into the "Ultimate Embarrassment." We made it through the evening with no further incident, and never, *ever* ventured into the world of art again—as artists, that is.

It's a work of art? Really?

Since then I have seriously tried to understand modern art. But it seems that when I try to get through a *Time* magazine article about some traveling art show in the country, my eye inadvertently wanders to the nearest political cartoon.

My 26-year-old son is much more savvy about contemporary art than I am. Therefore, when he came to visit me last summer, we took the Metro to Washington, D.C., where we "surfaced" at the Smithsonian Institution. Among others, we visited the Hirshhorn Museum and Sculpture Garden.

I should have done more homework before I went, because I couldn't make heads or tails of most of what I saw there. Some of the framed works were identified as "Portrait of [someone]." But I must admit that all those Picasso-like, disjointed body parts and runny splotches of color thrown across the canvases just didn't "say" anything to me. I did my best to *look* like a connoisseur of fine art, which includes standing for a long time close to a picture, and then standing back a ways, cocking one's head to the left and then the right.

At one point in our self-guided tour, my son and I became separated briefly. Looking about for him, I happened to glance at another visitor who just then happened to glance at me. We both quickly looked back at the confusing work in question, then cautiously back at each other. From the intensity of her previous gaze at the portrait, I was sure she understood what she was seeing and I didn't want to embarrass myself. Straining for what I hoped was a deeply cerebral expression in my eyes, I thoughtfully nodded my head and allowed a spontaneous "H'mmm" to escape my throat. The woman stared at me. I suppose I was expecting some type of a connoisseurial "connecting" smile to pass between us and waited for the unspoken, magical moment.

Instead, the woman unexpectedly rolled her eyes as if I were some kind of fool and emitted a condescending laugh-snort before brushing past me toward the exit. Well, at least she was more honest about her feelings than I had been.

My aunt, the artist

Someone in my family who really understands art is my aunt. When she was finally able to retire and take a little time for herself, Aunt Evelyn took up oil painting—and became successful at it almost immediately. Although her arts and crafts-style Scandinavian castles, impressionistic fruit and flower still lifes, airy ballerinas, and Oriental depictions are breathtaking, she has made the greatest name for herself in animal portraiture. Her many commissions have included lapdogs, hunting breeds, and even one man's prizewinning bull.

I am amazed at how accurately my gifted aunt can portray so many aspects of life in so many different painting styles. Walking through the rooms of her home is like walking through an art gallery.

My favorite gifts from Aunt Evy are paintings she's done. When she gives me a painting of hers, she gives me part of herself. She has visualized the subject of the art piece. She herself has chosen the colors with which to bring it to life. Her personality and individual stamp are part of that picture. That's what makes the gift so meaningful.

The artist's palette

When my aunt begins to paint the likeness of someone's pet, she first goes through her tubes of paint and selects the colors she wants. Next, onto her palette she squeezes seemingly random splotches of color. Then she begins painting, picking up a drop of color from the palette and dabbing it onto the canvas—again and again.

Eventually, a likeness emerges. It blows me away every time! When Cher and I jammed our brushes haphazardly into colored paint back in college and then splashed them onto a background, the result was chaos. I don't understand how Aunt Evy can transfer random blobs of colored oil from her palette onto a canvas with such perfect, exact placements (thousands of them!) that a perfect likeness of the subject in the photograph appears on her previously blank canvas. Amazing!

A personal palette

A woman growing into the beauty of holiness also has a palette of colors that the Master Artist has placed within her reach. Which colors she decides to use in the completion of her portrait is an individual choice. The colors on her palette are the gifts of the Spirit God has given each of us. These include the gentle shades of love, joy, peace, and long-suffering (Gal. 5:22, 23). The selection on the palette also include other shades from which she can choose: forgiveness, discipline, tolerance, and balance, among others.

The Master Artist has also provided a how-to-paint manual that she can consult on the proper use of colors in her portrait.

"Bible religion is not one influence among many others; its influence is to be supreme, pervading and controlling every other. It is not to be like a dash of color brushed here and there upon the canvas, but it is to pervade the whole life, as if the canvas were dipped into the color, until every thread of the fabric were dyed a deep, unfailing hue."[1]

C. S. Lewis commented, "The Bible, read in the right spirit . . . will bring us to Him."[2]

The chapters that follow will look more closely at how to apply some of the shades on the Master's palette, as well as portrait restoration, if colors from the counterfeit palette have been used in the painting.

---

[1] E. G. White, *The Desire of Ages*, p. 312.

[2] C. S. Lewis, in *The Quotable Lewis*, p. 72.

CHAPTER 17

SHE LOOKS FORGIVEN: OF CARBONATE AND CRYSTAL

Forgive as the Lord forgave you.
—Colossians 3:13, NIV

I think that if God forgives us we must forgive ourselves. Otherwise it is almost like setting up ourselves as a higher tribunal than Him.
—C. S. Lewis

One color that is difficult to apply to one's portrait—and make it stick—is forgiveness. And yet, in a well-painted portrait, a beautiful woman does look forgiving.

"There is no use in talking as if forgiveness were easy," writes C. S. Lewis. "For we find that the work of forgiveness has to be done over and over again."[1] Perhaps it is because God forgives us again and again that forgiveness is our heavenly Parent's most endearing trait to His children (after unconditional love). "What God has done for us in Christ is to say through His forgiveness that we are valuable, individually important—even when we sin."[2]

King David, who had all but ruined his portrait with the dark blotches of adultery and murder, implored, "Look upon mine affliction and my pain; and forgive all my sins" (Ps. 25:18). Later he exclaimed with relief, "You are forgiving and good, O Lord, abounding in love to all who call to you" (Ps. 86:5, NIV). Years later Daniel echoed this assurance: "The Lord our God is merciful and forgiving, even though we have rebelled against him" (Dan. 9:9, NIV).

Forgiveness is what Calvary is all about. Paul, especially, pointed out this fact. "God exalted him [Christ] to his own right hand as Prince and Savior that he might give repentance and forgiveness of sins to Israel" (Acts 5:31, NIV).

But Scripture makes it very clear that God's willingness to forgive us is dependent upon our willingness to forgive those who have wronged us. "Bear with each other and forgive whatever grievances you may have against one another. Forgive as the Lord forgave you" (Col. 3:13, NIV).

Christ clarified this divine principle immediately following His example prayer (commonly known as the Lord's Prayer): "For if you forgive men when they sin against you, your heavenly Father will also forgive you. But if you do not forgive men their sins, your Father will not forgive your sins" (Matt. 6:14, 15, NIV).

It's hard! It's hard! It's hard!

Why did God make His gift of forgiveness of our sins contingent on our forgiving others—especially when so many of His other gifts (e.g., love, sunshine and rain, the Holy Spirit) have no strings attached? Perhaps He knows how difficult it is for humans to forgive. Even after living with Jesus for months, John and James, the "sons of thunder," would still rather have called down fire from heaven on Christ's enemies than forgive them. In the upper room the evening before the Crucifixion Peter was arguing about how forgiveness works. And that even while the Master knelt before him, holding a servant's basin containing clean water, a symbol of forgiveness.

A friend of mine (I'll call her Becky) shared with me her own "upper room" experience. Becky found herself alone after her husband of more than 20 years had an affair with one of her friends, Doreen. Shattered beyond words, Becky numbly went through the motions of living for the next few months. At the end of each day she was amazed that she had "made it" another 24 hours. Going to church every week, however, was the hardest, for Doreen attended her church as well.

Intellectually Becky had forgiven her estranged husband as well as Doreen, with whom she had once conversed by phone after news of the affair had become public domain. Becky knew that "hostility and an unforgiving spirit are acids which destroy our capacity to worship and pray."[3] But every time she saw Doreen at church, she felt as if a bitter sword were again cutting into her heart. To avoid having to see Doreen—even in her peripheral vision—she developed the habit of sitting in a pew near the front of the church.

In the upper room

Looking at the church bulletin one Sabbath morning, she realized that this day the congregation would take Communion after the ordinance of humility (also known as footwashing).

God, Becky prayed in sudden panic, *I certainly hope You aren't expecting me to wash the feet of you-know-who! Remember that I have forgiven her already. So let's just leave it at that, shall we?*

During the opening song, the collection of tithes and offerings, and the special music, she continued wrestling with God. Then the pastor rose to speak. Included in his homily was the text "And when ye stand praying, forgive, if ye have ought against any: that your Father also which is in heaven may forgive you your trespasses" (Mark 11:25).

Lord, Becky begged, struggling to hold back frustrated tears, *You know I've forgiven her the best I can. I'm just waiting for my emotions to catch up with my moral choice. I don't want to be anywhere near her. But if You show me You want me to wash her feet, I guess I'll do it.*

At the close of his homily, the pastor dismissed the congregation to wash one another's feet. When an elderly friend approached Becky, asking her to be her footwashing partner, Becky accepted with a silent *Thank You, Lord!*

The woman led Becky to one of the rooms where women had gathered and were already singing. Becky's wary eyes quickly surveyed the occupants. No Doreen. *Thank You, Lord! She must have gone to another room.*

"I'll wash your feet first, dear," said Becky's partner.

When the woman had finished, Becky said, "I'll take the basin up front and get clean water."

Because of the crowded room, it was necessary that the women form two lines from opposite sides of the room. The heads of each line converged at a small table, where a deaconess dispensed clean towels and fresh water alternately to women in the two lines.

Foot—and heart—washing

Relaxed and singing with the others, Becky waited at the head of her line to be served. She had just emptied the used water from her basin into a large bucket when the woman at the head of the other line stepped away. With horror and a sudden stab of unspeakable pain, Becky found herself suddenly staring into the face of Doreen, who quickly jerked her chin down into her shoulder.

In that instant, Becky told me, though she was tempted to drop the basin and run, she was held motionless by the anguish and shame all over Doreen's face. Her heart went out to the former friend by whom she had been so deeply betrayed. She suddenly heard a whispered "Doreen" escape her own lips. Hesitating, Doreen looked up, and their eyes met.

At that instant the deaconess ladled fresh, clean water into Becky's basin.

"It sounded like a bubbling mountain stream," she told me, "and I felt as if God were washing away the bitter residue still lingering in my heart. Then and there He helped me forgive Doreen in every way possible, and a ton of bricks came off my shoulders."

The following week Doreen wrote Becky a letter asking her forgiveness and expressing her grief over the part she'd played in breaking up Becky's marriage. Later the two women met, reestablished ties, and parted after a tearful embrace.

To be forgiven . . .

A beautiful woman looks not only forgiving, but also *forgiven*. Why is it that some of us, who may not have much trouble forgiving others, can hardly forgive ourselves—or even accept God's forgiveness for our sins? Perhaps that was part of Peter's personal dilemma in the upper room.

Carrying one's own guilt around is an incredible burden. "The heaviest burden that we bear is the burden of sin. If we were left to bear this burden, it would crush us. . . . He [Christ] will take the load from our weary shoulders. . . . He invites us to cast all our care upon Him; for He carries us upon His heart."[4]

Exchanging our guilt for His forgiveness brings joy and peace of mind. The first thing Christ said to a palsied man He was about to heal was "Son, *be of good cheer*; thy sins be forgiven thee" (Matt. 9:2).

Drugs and sex

"But you don't know everything I've done—how could God forgive me?" the young woman asked, her brown eyes tearful.

We had been randomly seated at the same table for the evening meal and musical program during a nondenominational Christian women's retreat held at a large hotel in the San Francisco Bay Area. When the conference president announced after the benediction that the printed postsession counseling time should have been placed under the next day's schedule of events, my new friend had become quite agitated. As the crowd of 800 amiably visiting women slowly found their way out of the chandeliered ballroom, Gina (not her real name) dissolved into tears.

Fatigued, I was eager to get back to my hotel room and hit the sack, but Gina's outburst kept me uneasily in my chair. I felt very awkward.

"I need a counselor. They promised counselors tonight! What am I going to do?"

Some of the women, nearly immobile in the slowly exiting crowd, cast curious glances in our direction.

Gina leaned toward me and whispered, "I'm suffering from every addiction known to man—including sex!" Another burst of tears was followed by sniffles. She tried in vain to dry her eyes with her hands. I handed her a tissue and wondered why she was unloading all of this on me.

"I feel so dirty! I've asked forgiveness so many times, but somehow end up doing the same old stuff again. When that quartet ended with 'Whiter Than Snow,' I knew that all I'd ever want in life anymore was just to be clean. Oh, I just want to be clean!" Then laying her head on her arms, she gave herself up to great heaving sobs.

I'd never seen someone in such emotional and spiritual despair, and was deeply moved.

What do I do now?

Not being a counselor, I just sat there like a dummy, feeling totally helpless. Should I get help? Should I hold Gina's hand? My mind was so confused! A couple attendants who had begun busing the tables near us cast uneasy glances in our direction as they clanked dirty tableware into large plastic containers.

I asked God if I should say something or just keep my mouth shut. Hearing no distinct "answer," I finally decided to make a clumsy—but prayerful—stab at it.

"Oh, Gina—oh, baby, I'm so, *so* sorry. You're really hurting, aren't you? Would you like me to try to find one of the counselors for you?"

"No—" Sobs cut short her words. I waited, and she spoke again. "I'm too much of a mess right now. Just talk to me, *please!* Give me *some* kind of hope!" Drying her eyes, she looked at me expectantly.

I swallowed, battling an empathetic lump in my throat. "From what you said, Gina, I can tell you believe in God. And I think He believes in you. You wouldn't have come to this conference unless it was His love drawing you here."

Her eyes begged for comfort. I struggled on.

"Have you ever heard of the promise in the Bible that says 'If we confess our sins, he is faithful and just to forgive us our sins, and to cleanse us from all unrighteousness' [1 John 1:9]?"

"Yes," she answered with a nod of recognition. "My parents are church people and have tried to help me. It's just so hard to believe God could do something with me after all the gross stuff I've done. That would take a miracle!"

A miracle

"That's a beautiful ring you're wearing," I said suddenly.

"Thanks," she responded through sniffles and looked down at her hand. "My father gave it to me for my birthday. I think it's some kind of crystal or something."

"Do you know how crystal is formed?" I asked her.

"No, not really. Do you?"

"Yes, kind of. I gave guided tours in a cave once and had to explain to visitors about crystal formations. I guess you could say that crystal is formed by a miracle, of sorts. At least part of that crystal in your ring started out as a clear, pure raindrop—like you started out, clean and pure."

She nodded sadly, still looking at her ring.

"That little raindrop possibly fell onto a muddy, dead leaf above a cave somewhere. Gravity probably pulled it off the leaf. It was dirty as it drifted down through the topsoil with the other raindrops. The farther it went, the dirtier it got. It might even have passed through the decomposing flesh of a partially buried squirrel carcass. It probably picked up some contaminated substances and even absorbed some pretty rotten odors—I can't believe I'm giving a cave lecture in the ballroom of the Marriott!" I interjected suddenly with a little laugh.

"It's OK," she reassured me, smiling. "Please go on."

"All right. The formless muddy moisture that once had been a clean raindrop picked up carbon dioxide from pockets of air around decaying vegetation and sank even farther into the ground. As it passed through clammy corridors and strange underground pressures, it began to lose some of the 'dirtiness' it had passed through. And as it traveled its unpredictable path, the carbon dioxide began working in the raindrop, and something known as carbonic acid—the stuff that puts bubbles in 7-Up—slowly began dissolving the limestone beneath it. Some of *this* solution became part of the raindrop.

"A miracle, of sorts, was taking place. For when this dissolved limestone solution reached the warmer air inside the cavern, it released crystals—not ones that smelled of rotted vegetation or particles of mud and impurity. No, these crystals of calcium carbonate were pure, even to the point of being transparent."

Gina had been moving her hand, watching the light reflect off the polished sides of the crystal in her ring.

"Gina, I guess this is what I'm getting at."

She looked up at me.

"Just as God—who created beautiful, clean raindrops, as well as beautiful, clean girls [she smiled at me slightly]—planned an underground miracle to turn dirty raindrops into jewels, that same God has a miracle to make you cleaner and more beautiful than you ever dreamed."

Gina reached for my hands. "Oh, Carolyn, the two things I want most in life are to be pure again, and then, someday, to know—with a husband—what *pure* love really is." Tears flooded her eyes again as she said, "I've decided to get professional help again. Would you pray for me?"

Against a background of clanking tableware being set out on the tables for breakfast and conversation of custodians vacuuming the carpet, I haltingly prayed for Gina as she clung to my hands and wept anew.

The morning after

I was the last person of my group to arrive at our assigned table the next morning for breakfast. Gina, engaged in animated discussion with one of the other women, was already seated on the far side of the large circular table. On my breakfast plate was a small white envelope. I discreetly opened it and read the following:

"Dear New Friend, Thank you for your time and prayer last night. I want you to know that today I am 'whiter than snow.' I think I finally forgave myself. With God's help, I'm going back into counseling. With His help, I will stay away from singles bars and liquor marts and do whatever I have to do to stay clean. Would you let me write you or leave an occasional phone message so that I have someone to be accountable to? Here's my address as well. Thanks again. Last night was a turning point. Pray for me. Love, Gina."

Damaged canvases

We have all taken colors from a palette other than the Master's and damaged the portrait we are painting. But the wonderful Master Artist is also an expert at portrait restoration.

"Do not remember the former things, or consider the things of old," He counsels us. "I am about to do a new thing" (Isa. 43:18, 19, NRSV). And this is the real miracle: "I, I am He who blots out your transgressions for my own sake, and I will not remember your sins" (verse 25, NRSV).

[1] C. S. Lewis, in *The Quotable Lewis,* p. 221.

[2] W. B. Hunter, *The God Who Hears,* p. 144.

[3] *Ibid.,* p. 147.

[4] E. G. White, *The Desire of Ages,* pp. 328, 329.

CHAPTER 18

SHE LOOKS DISCIPLINED: A MOUSE IN THE HOUSE

I urge you . . . to present your bodies a living and holy sacrifice, acceptable to God, which is your spiritual service of worship.
—Romans 12:1

I have often recoiled at the term disciplined, *for it implies sacrifice.*
—Carolyn Rathbun

In his new book, *Surrender, the Secret to Perfect Peace and Happiness*, pastor-author Gregory L. Jackson suggests that instead of having a "sacrifice" mentality when it comes to giving our wills over to God, we might do better by adopting a "surrender" outlook. "What God wants is to occupy first place in our hearts. He wants us to surrender all to Him—our will, our time, our energy, our plans, our desires, our goals, our loved ones—*all* to His control. . . . The cross is for dying, not for carrying. It is a symbol of dying to self so that God may have His rightful place in our lives."[1]

"As we lift this cross," writes Ellen White, "we shall find that it lifts us."[2]

Disciplined choices involve a gutsy effort to keep our wills on the side of God in every issue of our lives. "Discipline," writes Bill Hybels, "is one of the most important character qualities a person can possess. It plays a key role in developing every area of life."[3]

I often find that discipline in the areas of the "blacker" sins isn't difficult at all. It's in the dark corners of one's life—those besetting pet sins and habits—where self-discipline is the hardest. Perhaps that's because discipline in minor arenas doesn't seem that important to us. I'd have to admit I have felt that way—until a most frustrating encounter with a small gray mouse changed my thinking.

Tell-tail signs

Having lived in Africa for years, I learned to become very aggressive in dealing with mammoth cockroaches, malaria mosquitoes, bedbugs, snakes, and huge rats. Therefore, I should have acted decisively when I first suspected that a mouse had visited my third-story apartment in the relatively civilized state of California.

But, I rationalized, *I keep a fairly clean apartment, and the landlady has exterminators in regularly to deal with that sort of problem, so everything must be under control.* So I chose to do nothing.

Three weeks later I thought I saw more signs that a mouse had been in my kitchen. This time I grew uncomfortable and resolved to pick up rat poison that evening on the way home from school. But going from my car to the store, I had to walk by Pizza Hut. The aroma of hot melted cheese and tomato sauce drew me in. By the end of the meal I felt too relaxed to compete with do-it-yourselfers crowding the hardware store aisles, and simply went home instead.

Just as well, too, I decided, because no further evidence of a visiting mouse was visible. The next day I left to visit my parents over Thanksgiving vacation.

The fur thickens

As I walked into my apartment after the long weekend, I noticed a small area of carpet just outside the guest bedroom's closed door. Something had been chewing on the carpet! Looking toward the living room, I saw a gaping hole, six inches in diameter, in the center of the rocking chair cushion. Stuffing was strewn over the edge of the chair and onto the carpet below. Turning toward the kitchen, I saw mouse droppings all along the floor and the counter. Gross me out!

With my skin beginning to crawl, I cleaned up the mess and got right on the phone, leaving a message for the apartment manager to contact the exterminators. Then I got back in the car and drove down to Builder's Emporium to buy mousetraps. I didn't get one of those open-to-the-public kind in which the trapped mouse gets killed and lies exposed, waiting for burial. Oh, no! I wanted no contact with the creature. So, paying $10 more, I purchased a couple high-tech models in two sizes: big and bigger.

At different locations in my apartment I propped them up with their little doors open. I reasoned that when the mouse entered one of these traps in search of the aromatic bait, the trap would be bumped, the door would slam shut, and I'd never even have to see the creature or its final anguish.

My colleagues at school gave me all kinds of advice prior to the faculty meeting.

"Use rat poison," the history teacher advised me.

"No," disagreed the biology professor. "Rat poison contaminates the air."

"Well," intoned the office secretary, "I've lived in a lot of places, and you can't beat that old standby—cheese."

"What? Cheese never works!" argued the principal. "With rodents, it's peanut butter. It's foolproof—they go for it every time!"

I didn't tell any of them I'd left raisins in the traps.

Arriving home that evening, I was disheartened to find both traps sprung—but empty. And *more* carpet had been chewed up. My apartment was taking on a sinister air.

Confrontation

Then while I was just standing there, something streaked out from under the couch and shot beneath the refrigerator. Quickly I shut the bedroom and bathroom doors. Then nonchalantly whistling, I walked over to the couch, slipped my banjo strap over my shoulder, and sat down. In full control of my emotions I began playing "Foggy Mountain Breakdown." I would show that mouse that I could play the waiting game too.

At that point I suddenly learned something I hadn't known before: either mice have very sensitive eardrums that plucked banjo strings intensely irritate, or mice don't like "Foggy Mountain Breakdown."

Whatever the case, this mouse came flying out from under the refrigerator in a panic and began racing in circles atop the living area carpet. In a frenzy it tore down the short hallway and began throwing its tiny body against the closed door of the guest room.

That dealing-with-wild-varmint cool I'd developed in Africa suddenly deserted me. All I can truthfully recall is that I was suddenly standing by the front door, madly jogging in place, *still* playing "Foggy Mountain Breakdown," and repeatedly yelling at the frantic mouse, "Oh, no, you don't!"

Then the mouse made a break for it and disappeared under the couch. Trembling, I grabbed a broom. With the heavy banjo still hanging from my neck, I got down on my knees and jabbed the broom handle around under the couch, but the creature seemed to have disappeared within its deep recesses.

Snatching up my purse, I sped to the supermarket, where I purchased a cheap, efficient, show-all mouse trap and the most smelly deli cheese I could find.

Second thoughts

Baiting the "death machine" in front of the refrigerator door, I had mixed emotions. You see, the mouse I had seen wasn't some big, repulsive rat. It was a little, *very* cute creature that had the healthy, shiny fur of a mother-to-be.

Nevertheless, my brief empathetic maternal feelings changed when I retired for the night to my bedroom and found that one end of a lovely gift rug had been completely chewed up and the carpet beneath badly soiled.

After cleaning up this *latest* mess and feeling as if my apartment were turning into a slum dwelling, I laid despondently in bed and wondered why on earth I hadn't done something about the mouse when I'd first suspected its presence. In four short weeks it had taken over my house, and my life, and was now preparing to reproduce itself at an unknown location under *my* roof.

Letting out a beleaguered sigh, I noticed the message light flashing on my answering machine. Ah! The landlady had called earlier to tell me that exterminators would be up to my apartment the next day. *Thank You!*

Resolution

The following morning, while replacing a milk carton in the refrigerator, I kicked something—the mousetrap with a stranglehold on a very pregnant (and very dead) mouse. With a feeling of utter revulsion, I grabbed my briefcase and ran out the door, leaving the mouse mess for the exterminators. But that afternoon the landlady called me at school to inform me the exterminators would not be able to get to my place until the *next* day.

So in the end, poetic justice was served. I had no choice but to go home and deal with the mouse that *I* had nurtured in my home by not taking early, decisive action against it.

The mouse may be gone, but its memory lives on. And here is what its memory has taught me. One bad habit or besetting sin that I tolerate in my life is like that cute little mouse. It can infiltrate, damage, and eventually contaminate the rest of my spiritual "house." Left unchallenged, it will become a part of me.

Steven Mosley cites studies done by Dr. Elden Chalmers of Loma Linda University and D. Deane Walcott of UCLA, who report that repeated behaviors actually make pathways in the central nervous system: "Thoughts and words and actions become a permanent part of the brain." Mosley concludes, "The longer a habit persists, the more our minds become a Gothic edifice full of hidden passageways and trapdoors where we can ignore the obvious and postpone the inevitable."[4]

Mousetraps

Using biblical principles, Mosley provides the reader with proven strategies for taking detours around these established pathways in order to overcome besetting sins and habits. I have found this book to be extremely helpful on a practical, as well as a spiritual, level.

What follows are five of Mosely's "mousetraps" that a woman of beauty can "set" in order to keep her dwelling free from contamination.

First, realize that you are not your habit.[5] Your habit is your habit, but you are a child of God. Instead of spending time focusing on the besetting sin, focus on where you want to go with God.

Second, consciously put your will on God's side, inviting Him to come into the midst of your problem and work with you from the inside out.[6] Philippians 2:12, 13 states: "Work out your own salvation with fear and trembling. For it is God which worketh in you both to will and to do of his good pleasure." When temptation calls you to "come out and play," that is the exact moment to give God a call: "Daddy, put Your arms around me!" Our Father, who hears each sincere plea, will answer our cries.

A third strategy is to avoid situations and places that are familiar settings for besetting sins and pernicious habits. These might include the bakery section of a supermarket, the irresistible hunk on a soap opera, the end of the mall near the store whose credit card you carry, certain aisles of the video store, or simply returning in your mind to the watering trough of resentment for others' past wrongs toward you.

Determine not to start a new day unless you're "armed to the teeth," as Mosley puts it, with memorized phrases, verses, or passages that speak strength to one's weakest areas.

"Don't duel with temptation; overwhelm it with the Word."[7] That is precisely what Christ did at the end of His 40 days in the wilderness.

Finally, celebrate your successes with God. No one, even those heavily involved in church work or in the loving care of others, is safe from a "mouse in the house." Even Paul described what he did in order to avoid giving in to a besetting sin: "But I keep under my body, and bring it into subjection: lest that by any means, when I have preached to others, I myself should be a castaway" (1 Cor. 9:27).

May God grant us the moral strength beautiful women need in order to discipline their lives in such a way that a "mouse" will never be able to survive in her "house."

---

[1] Gregory L. Jackson, *Surrender, the Secret to Perfect Peace and Happiness* (Hagerstown, Md.: Review and Herald Pub. Assn., 1994), p. 19.

[2] E. G. White, *Testimonies for the Church* (Mountain View, Calif.: Pacific Press Pub. Assn., 1904), vol. 8, p. 45.

[3] Bill Hybels, *Who You Are When No One's Looking* (Downers Grove, Ill.: Inter-Varsity Press, 1987), p. 24.

[4] Steven Mosley, *There I Go Again* (Dallas: Word Publishing, 1991), p. 23.

[5] *Ibid.,* p. 51.

[6] *Ibid.,* pp. 34-48.

[7] *Ibid.,* pp. 84-96.

CHAPTER 19

SHE LOOKS TRUSTING: FAT GIVES!

In quietness and trust is your strength.
—Isaiah 30:15, NIV

Trust in the Lord with all your heart and
lean not on your own understanding.
—Proverbs 3:5, NIV

Back to the ceiling,
Belly to the floor—
Looks like this crawl's
Gonna go some more.

So go the somewhat altered lyrics of Fred Stork's cave ballad. The setting portrayed in this song described perfectly my physical situation when I called out to Margaret.

"Could you help me, please?" Attempting to cut the edge of panic out of my voice I added, "I think I'm stuck!"

I was just learning how to be a spelunker and was with a group of weekend cavers from the Sacramento chapter of the National Speleological Society. We were exploring Ripple Cave, named for the distinctive rippled calcite flowstone on some of its walls. Margaret, an experienced caver, was giving me a personal tour of the upper part of the cave. Although I was somewhat smaller than my new friend, I was still having problems getting through "The Connection" that she'd wriggled through so easily.

"How did you do it?" I panted, trying not to hyperventilate as I fought back panic.

In order to get to dry cavern rooms, known as bedroom chambers, we were having to squeeze on our bellies through this connecting passage. The short passage itself looked like a lopsided triangular hole. It would have been more manageable if the "bottom" of the triangle hadn't been a sharply sloping slab that abruptly ended a few inches from the wall.

"Turn your head sideways," Margaret suggested.

I laid my head down on my right cheek and extended my right arm so the top part of my body could push more easily through the wet sand and shallow puddles. Lying flat on the sloping slab, I dropped the toes of my hiking boots into what sounded like a puddle, and attempted to push against its slimy base.

A rough formation hanging from the top of the triangle dug into my back. Straining forward, I felt it let go of my spine and then catch the soaked pocket of my industrial-strength coveralls. For an instant it held me fast. Then forcing my hipbone over a nub on the rocky surface beneath, I heard my pocket rip.

Slip-sliding away . . .

That's when I started sliding over the one and a half inches of open space to my left. In two seconds my entire left side, from knee to shoulder, had fallen neatly and securely into the space between the slanted triangle's floor and the rough wall. I was helplessly pinned.

As if that weren't bad enough, during the slide the cord of my electric headlamp caught on a projection of granite and yanked my helmet down over my face, plunging me into total darkness and giving me only used air to breathe. Normally I am not prone to claustrophobia, but right then . . .

"Margaret!" I emitted a muffled cry from the inside of the helmet.

"You're just fine," she said calmly, "but we might have to work on this a little bit. . . . Let's see now."

I lay there, tensing to keep from sinking even more into the granite trap, and cave entrapment stories floated through my mind. Back in 1925 Floyd Collins, now a caving legend, had been trapped by a small rock in a Kentucky cave. Would-be rescuers took turns bringing him hot drinks and sandwiches. His lifeless body was removed two months after he had gotten trapped.[1] I also recalled a caving friend explaining why cave rescue is the slowest form of rescue.

"You can't get a helicopter down into a cave," he'd said, "or even a stretcher, if it's a narrow passage. So cave safely."

My left leg slipped another half inch into the cave's vicelike grip. I tensed up even more.

"OK, I got it now," said Margaret, confidently. "The first thing you need to do is relax."

"Not possible," I objected. Whenever I relaxed, my left side slid into the granite and calcite trap even more. And already, when I strained the muscles in an attempt to push, the cold stone seemed almost to cut into the muscles.

"Relax," said Margaret firmly.

"But Margaret," I whimpered from inside the helmet that was still clamped over my perspiring face, "I can't even see you, and I don't feel so good." At this point I really didn't care if she thought I was a wimp. I was only 43 and still had a lot of life to live.

"In other words," she said thoughtfully through the darkness, "you can get out of this by yourself and don't need my advice anymore?"

"*No-o-o!*"

"Oh, so you *do* need my help. For starters, use your extended right hand to pull the helmet off your face."

The rush of cool, relatively fresh air gave me a burst of relief.

"Now, once again, Carolyn, I want you to *relax.*"

She *still* didn't get it.

"I told you I'd drop down more if I did that." My voice was sounding weak.

Friendly fat cells

"Good!" she responded. "The sooner, the better. When your muscles are tense, you have more body mass. But when you relax them, your body mass seems to be a whole lot more fat. All experienced cavers know that . . . fat gives! Remember that."

In an act of great irony, I mustered all the strength I had and focused my energy on . . . relaxing. Just as I feared, my shoulder slipped down even farther, as did my hipbone and thigh. But my previously pinned arm and knee dropped all the way through. I felt like a baby on the edge of a table with one arm and leg dangling off.

"Arm and leg fell through," I informed my guide.

"Good!" Margaret responded. "Now find irregularities in the wall against which you can use your free leg and arm to push. Then relax and give yourself a little push up and over. When you can't go any farther, stop, relax, and repeat the process."

So I followed instructions as she called them out to me. *Relax. Push. Stop. Relax. Push. Stop.* No one had said that to me since the day I gave birth to our son. But this time it felt as if *I* were in the birth canal.

Sooner than I would have believed (but still not soon enough), my weary upper body pulled the rest of me out the other side of "The Connection." I could have saved myself much anxiety and energy had I just followed the wise advice of my cave guide the first time she gave it to me.

Panic or peace

In addition to fat, something else that needed to "give" before I could move forward through "The Connection" was self-dependency. Granted, as I struggled in my own willfulness, I *was* moving, but sideways, backward, and downhill—in an out-of-control slide. Acting on the wisdom of my guide, however (even if emotion and logic were telling me to do the exact opposite), gave my movements direction, control, and energy.

In making our way through life's dark tunnels, why is it we so often feel that our thrashing movements will have more merit than relaxing into a trusting wait for God to call out the directions? "Worry is blind, and cannot discern the future; but Jesus sees the end from the beginning. In every difficulty He has His way prepared to bring relief. Our heavenly Father has a thousand ways to provide for us, of which we know nothing."[2]

> "O what peace we often forfeit,
> O what needless pain we bear,
> All because we do not carry
> Everything to God in prayer."[3]

A beautiful woman is learning through every crisis and deficiency in her life to "rest in the Lord" (Ps. 37:7).

Trapped in Rattlesnake Canyon

If relaxing is the first step toward trust, then leaning by faith on the arm of God is the next one. And this second step can be as difficult a decision to make as was the first. How ironic that our fears sometimes keep us from trusting the only One who can help us through our difficulties to firmer spiritual, emotional, and even financial ground.

Hiking and bouldering my way up Rattlesnake Canyon in Joshua Tree National Monument with my brother, his two children, and my child one afternoon, I found myself trapped on a sharply sloping rock overhang right below the canyon's rim. My back was wedged into a V-shaped joint that rose a foot above my head. I watched as my worn-smooth tennies slipped—first one, and then the other—on the slick granite slope.

My brother, an experienced climber, pulled himself up onto the shallow granite platform. His long arms spanned the wide sides of the V. How much safer I felt having him stand between me and a 1,500-foot fall. Then he said something I didn't want to hear.

"Let go of your handholds," he instructed, "and trade places with me. That way I can boost you up over the top."

I said nothing and continued clinging to my two puny handholds.

"Relax. I've got my arm around you," he explained patiently. "You're not going anyplace. But the next move is yours. You can let go so we can change position and I'll be able to help you over the top. Or you can keep holding on to your handholds and stay here for the rest of your life."

With my legs feeling like wet noodles, I finally chose to lean against my brother's left arm and let go of my handholds. After we had traded places, and with his left arm still about me, he helped wedge my right foot between his right knee and the V-shaped wall.

"Good!" he encouraged. "Now put your whole weight on the foot I'm supporting."

I cautiously followed his directions, and suddenly there I was—crawling onto the flat, safe rocks bordering the top of the canyon. It had happened so quickly and with so little effort on my part.

Learning to lean

God wants us not only to relax, but also to lean on His strong arm. He asked Job, "Do you have an arm like God" (Job 40:9, NASB)? Luke affirmed, "He has done mighty deeds with His arm" (Luke 1:51, NASB).

And gentle is the strong arm of God. "Behold," wrote Isaiah, "the Lord God will come with might, with His arm ruling for Him. . . . Like a shepherd He will tend His flock, in His arm He will gather the lambs" (Isa. 40:10, 11, NASB).

In His human form, Jesus relaxed and leaned on His Father's arm. "I can do nothing on My own initiative," He said. "I do not seek My own will, but the will of Him who sent me" (John 5:30, NASB).

FAT= f(aith) a(nd) t(rust)

Sometimes when I'm tempted to be overly self-dependent, or even self-protective, I have to remind myself that "fat (**faith and trust**) gives." Gives what? Gives one the peace of mind and the courage she needs in order to lean, with the weight of *all* her cares, on the strong arm of God.

---

¹ Donald Dale Jackson and the editors of Time-Life Books, *Underground Worlds* (Alexandria, Va.: Time-Life Books, 1982), pp. 101-103.

² E. G. White, *The Desire of Ages,* p. 330.

³ Charles C. Converse, "What a Friend We Have in Jesus," *The Seventh-day Adventist Hymnal,* No. 499.

CHAPTER 20

SHE LOOKS TOLERANT: "WHATH YO NAME?"

Comfort the feebleminded.
—1 Thessalonians 5:14

Tolerance and acceptance of those different from ourselves are hues lavishly used in the portrait of a beautiful woman. Someone once defined tolerance as "seeing things with your heart instead of your eyes." *

If someone is a fast learner, just one "special" person may be all it takes to open another's heart and mind. For the more stubborn among us, however, it might take a whole *group* of special people to teach tolerance and acceptance. Though I don't like admitting it, such was the case with me . . .

Moaning cavern

It's going to be one of those hot sun 'n' lizard days, I mused to myself, *but I'll stay cool down in the cave.*

I had never had such a wonderful summer job. Giving tours at this natural wonder and popular tourist attraction near Vallecito, California, was the best! Tucking in the stray tail of my blouse, I glanced at my carefully ironed guide uniform reflected in the Moaning Cavern gift shop window. Opening the door to the gift shop, I stepped in.

"Guess what, Carolyn?" Deena greeted me. "Your first tour this morning is a group of 25 mentally disabled adults on their way home from a week of camping. Good luck!"

I stopped in the doorway. "What? Wait a minute!" I yelled, but she had already hurried into the darkroom to develop a set of group photos.

It's not that I was prejudiced against mentally disabled people, you understand. It's just that they are so strange and unpredictable to be around. *OK,* I told myself, *let's think this through.* So far that summer I had, without too much stress, managed claustrophobic tourists, boisterous Boy Scouts, a young woman who fainted midway through the tour, and even a few squalling babies. But how would I ever get 25 uncoordinated, possibly dangerous, mentally disabled adults down—and then back up—236 steps on the cavern's see-through metal staircase? A day didn't pass when at least one "normal" visitor insisted on admiring the cave's exquisite beauty from the upper platform, instead of descending the spiral staircase to the floor.

I started to get a little scared as I waited for the group to arrive. I filled up my time by dusting around the cash register and rearranging merchandise on the gift shop shelves.

All too soon their white tour bus wound its way down the narrow road and into the gravel parking lot. Stepping onto the porch, I surveyed the situation. The driver backed out of the door at the front of the bus.

I'll bet he doesn't dare turn his back on them, I thought nervously. *And I'm supposed to lead them down the staircase? Ha! I just hope no one is carrying a knife!*

"Now listen up, everyone," he called from the front door. "Just keep your seats! Stay exactly where you are while I go buy the tickets."

I noticed several of the passengers, necks craned, staring out the windows at me. Feeling mild revulsion, I avoided their gaze and forced a smile at the driver coming up the steps.

"Well, we made it!" he beamed. "Where do I get the tickets?"

I pointed to the gift shop.

Soon he emerged and returned to the bus. "All right, everyone," he announced jovially. "Let's go see a cave!"

The passengers, some of them struggling clumsily, rose from their seats and jostled into the aisle of the bus.

Here we go

Here we go, I thought glumly. *Yippee* . . . How perfectly they fit my stereotypical image of what mentally disabled people look like. Some walked with abrupt, twitching movements; others looked about them with vacant stares. One man was drooling, and a partially blind man in his 20s, lightly rocking his head back and forth, clung to the arm of a male chaperon.

I couldn't help feeling sorry for the group's escorts, locked into this demanding (read *repulsive*) responsibility. One of the chaperons, a gray-haired woman in her late 50s, smiled at me. Sympathetically I returned her smile, thinking how hard it must be to keep up a pleasant front in her position. How embarrassed she must feel, always having to be with *these* people.

Into the gift shop they came, smelling like the smoke from a week's worth of campfires. I tried not to breathe. "This way, please," I announced in a nasal tone, and ushered them into the room housing the cave's original vertical drop, enclosed by a protective fence. *I hope no one tries to jump the fence!* I thought.

"So glad you could all come out to the cave today." I smiled mechanically, feeling a twinge of guilt at my lie. "This is the cave's original entrance," I began my lecture, trying not to look at the man who was drooling or at the young woman with Down's syndrome features, who was standing uncomfortably close to me.

I didn't understand how the middle-aged and elderly chaperons could seem so at ease.

"I hab a question"

"Are there any questions?" I paused, silently planning my strategy for getting this motley group down and back up the metal spiral staircase.

"Yeth, I hab a quethion," lisped a slightly built Hispanic man with thick eyeglasses. Then he stopped and looked about uncertainly.

"That's fine, Danny," the tall bus driver reassured him. "Ask your question."

An eager grin spread across Danny's face as he again focused on me. "Whath yo name?" he asked.

Smiling indulgently, I sighed. "My name is Carolyn. Now we are going to continue our tour down into the cave."

Two women in the group who understood what I said giggled with childlike excitement.

Tolerating

Cautiously we made our way to the upper platform in Moaning Cavern's Big Room, then down the spiral staircase. I noticed how carefully, how compassionately, the chaperons shepherded their challenging group, encouraging clumsy Hilda, complimenting Bob on how well he was lifting his feet, thanking Nancy for not complaining on the long trip down.

Funny, but I had never thought of this group as composed of individual personalities who answered to their own names. Although I no longer felt physically threatened by these visitors, I still found them unappealing. Again I wondered about the patience of their escorts. Why would a person in his or her right mind give up life's normal adventures and slow down to a child's pace—intellectually as well as physically—in order to care for people such as these?

At the bottom of Moaning Cavern's Big Room, an expanse large enough to contain the Statue of Liberty, I launched into the last part of my lecture, pointing out the 35-foot igloo, the suspended angel wings, the MGM lion, and other distinctive formations found in that roomy arena. Although I had been here dozens of times, the serenity and grandeur of the highly decorated cave chamber never failed to overpower me as I looked up at what resembled a vast crystal cathedral. It was always with reluctance that I brought every tour to an end.

Accepting

"Are there any questions before we go back up the staircase?" I asked one final time.

"What's your name?" asked a stringy-haired, oversized woman in a flower-print dress.

"It's Carolyn," I answered, and a sponsor winked at me good-naturedly. "Any other questions? Yes, Danny?"

"Whath yo name?" he asked, just as he had at the beginning of the tour.

"Danny," I answered, "you know what my name is. It's Carolyn." He grinned and nodded.

Just then the tall, nearly blind man, who had been clinging to his chaperon's arm ever since he'd entered the cave, released his hold and awkwardly pushed his way between Danny and the drooler. Walking unsteadily toward me, he stopped a few inches from my face. He leaned over and squinted into my eyes. "What's your name?" he asked.

I could smell the outdoors on his clothing. The entire group seemed taken back and waited in silence for my answer. I forced one last professional smile and sighed. "Why, it's Carolyn."

He looked back at the others and gleefully repeated, "Why, ith Carolyn." Then he added, "And she'th nithe." Without warning, he suddenly threw his arms wide and gave me a spontaneous bear hug.

Instinctively I returned his gesture with a quick squeeze. This unexpected encounter brought laughter from the group, and the drooling man even applauded. I found myself laughing with them.

As the blind man's chaperon stepped forward, taking his elbow, my prejudice against these gentle visitors evaporated.

"You're Carolyn," said the Down's syndrome woman, nodding approval.

I returned her nod.

Both Bob and Nancy told me "You're nice" when I assisted them on the steepest steps on our trip out of the cave. Hilda reached out and lightly touched me as I passed her puffing heavily on the way up the stairs.

I realized, with a bit of a start, that this group of disabled people had accepted me as one of their own. In spite of a technical lecture they probably hadn't understood. In spite of the steep staircase I'd led them down, and back up again. They had put up with my orders and demands on them and were treating *me* as a special person. Humbly I realized that the chaperons, by their example, and my guests, by their childlike affection, had just given me a rare, real-life lesson in tolerance and unconditional acceptance. And strangely, for the first time since beginning work that morning, I felt good—real good.

So are you!

Normally I said goodbye to my tour groups at the top of the cavern steps, when we emerged into the gift shop. This time I found myself following them out the door and watching as they boarded the bus.

Once again, I couldn't help noticing the courtesy with which the chaperons treated each individual as they helped the group members to their seats.

"You did very well in the cave!" announced the bus driver to his passengers, wiping his shiny forehead with a blue handkerchief. "Because you were so good," he continued with seemingly unflagging energy, "we are going to have a special picnic on the way home. How would you like that?"

Amid the group's approving chatter, he slid into the driver's seat, fastened his seat belt, and turned the key in the ignition.

Thoughtfully I leaned over the railing of the front porch while the bus turned around on the dusty gravel. I watched the vehicle lurch several times, gaining momentum as it rolled toward the parking lot entrance. I spotted Nancy's cherubic face, and the man who was blind, still aimlessly moving his head about.

"Goodbye! Goodbye!" several began calling.

"'Bye now," the bus driver cheerfully called out his window as they drove past.

"'Bye," I answered thoughtfully.

I could see Danny's frantic wave. "You're nithe!" he called out, chin lifted above his half-closed window.

"So are you, Danny!" I answered before my throat tightened. "So are you."

---

*E. C. McKenzie, ed., *14,000 Quips and Quotes* (Grand Rapids: Baker Book House, 1980), p. 51.

CHAPTER 21

SHE LOOKS BALANCED: BOTH HANDS WARM

There is a time for everything,
and a season for every activity under heaven.
—Ecclesiastes 3:1, NIV

A beautiful woman strives for the balance in her life that Jesus had in His, balance between the mental, physical, spiritual, and social. "And Jesus increased in wisdom and stature, and in favor with God and man" (Luke 2:52).

But times of stress—toddlers in the family, being overcommitted with church responsibilities, dealing with a major trauma that consumes one's emotional energy—can present a challenge to achieving balance.

In striving toward balance, but not "having yet attained," as Paul would say, I have discovered that journaling one's thoughts from time to time has been helpful in evaluating growth—the direction life is taking—and discovering what might be missing.

What follows are poetic reflections taken from a journal that has been chronicling the past few years of this woman's "journey to joy."

A glance back

Excerpts from this portion of my journal deal with accepting the reality of facing life alone.

Beneath the Patchwork Quilt

Beneath the patchwork quilt
I'd sometimes fight sleep
to listen to the ticking of the clock
metronomed with his deep-slumbered breathing—
head against his shoulder,
warm in his unconscious embrace—
like a fledgling
in its feathered nest—

But now, I lie awake
beneath the patchwork quilt

and feel the rythmic cadence of one heart
that tries—in vain, perhaps—
to pull on a couple more old memories
for a bit of added warmth.

into the wind
leaning into the wind
is not the easiest way
to go—
but sometimes
it's the only way
to get there

Learning to lean
Excerpts from this journal section give snapshot glimpses of the gradual transfer of trust from an earthly marital support to a heavenly One. See the first few verses of Isaiah 54.

paddling Partner
from the front
of the canoe
I played at paddling,
thinking to direct
my course—
while the
Master Oarsman,
behind,
gave direction
to my
clumsy strokes

anticipation
if only,
like inhaling mint vapor
before a morning's sip
or tightening bindings
before December's downhill run
or holding still the heart
before the first brush of a kiss—
if only, O Lord,
I would anticipate
Your quiet coming
with this same—
this breathless—
anticipation

post-divorce birthday
cold breeze blowing
dry leaves rolling
end over pointed end
down the empty street—

in search of warmth
i head for home,
for once i'm there
i'm not alone

waiting is
the Lord of time—
i'm in His heart
and He's in mine

so with the
Time Inventor near,
i celebrate
another year

Natural remedies
*Breathing fresh forest fragrances or briny sea breezes, and experiencing
their accompanying sights and sounds, can do much to restore one's emotional health and sense of balance.*

company
grass-green dragonfly
on this dreary day
lighting on my sandal—
i guess i'll let you stay

Hats
"You're walking through life
in the sun,"
Said my former pupil
(a budding dermatologist):
"For you I prescribe a hat."

"God, we have to get
hats," I said.
So we went to REI, God and I,
to shop for hats.
I bought an earth-tone brown felt
with a wide brim;

God selected cloudy-sky gray.

Now when we walk, God and I,
      we wear our hats.
I wear mine and
      it protects my face.
But when God wears His,
      it's big enough for the both of us.

Egret

White egret
      Your graceful S-shaped neck extended
As you peer into cobalt waters

A wise one, you—
      One of few who gaze
Beyond their own reflections

seagull sabbatical

buffeted by wicked winds
and flying low,
the wing-weary seagull
gives itself up
to the grasping,
white-capped swells

gives itself up—
to the roller-coaster billows
and tummy-tightening troughs—
even as I must fall
with the same weary abandon
into Your sea of strength

seasonal migration

Jesus, give me wings
and let my spirit soar
on autumn thermals of Your love
till i be cold no more.

i'll fly through indian summer,
cross winter's ice-torn sea,
and wing my way toward heaven—
and eternal spring with Thee.

Lesson plans
Helping others gain better equilibrium often contributes to better balance in our own lives. To my beloved students I attribute much of my positive mental health!

seashore sunrise
(or nurturing a reluctant learner)
I'd thought to stay
close by his shell
should he emerge
with time—
I didn't know
the spreading dawn
was *me* being drawn
from mine

Lifelong Learner
Young scholars now look up to me;
My lecture notes their pages fill.
Yet, if they only knew the truth—
It's at *their* feet I'm learning still.

superfluous[1]
a teacher
must work hard
at being
unnecessary

for the greatest reward
of all
is to be needed
no longer

two-course meal[2]
there
on the barren white surface
assorted magnets secure
assorted words from
assorted pupils—
nourishment on both sides
of the refrigerator door

Extracurricular

How difficult it is to find time for life's nonessentials—which perhaps should become more essential in computing our equation for personal balance.

Dobro
when i had
no more tears
to shed,
i bought
a Dobro . . .
to do
my crying
for me

banjo
cradled in the crook
of my arm,
random fingers roam
your fret board
until picked-out
plain-faced plucking
brings depression
to its knees

the perfect sandwich
the perfect sandwich
is
peanut butter
and
bluegrass jam

writing
writing
is like arranging clutter
in a roomful of words—
so the soul can unwind
in a well-ordered mind

Movin' on
We are to love our neighbors as much as we love ourselves. The following thoughts are about learning to accept and love one's self.

Permanent Residence
Wherever I may chance
to be,
I find that I reside
in me.

Holding Hands
The two of them I noticed
Sitting close in church
Holding tight hands,
Fingers intertwined.

Alone, I looked down
At hands folded in my lap
And noticed—
They were both warm.

hobo girl and Companion
God takes my pack,
we freely roam;
no matter where we are—
i'm home!

---

[1] Carolyn Rathbun, "Superfluous," *Delta Kappa Gamma Bulletin* 61, No. 1 (Fall 1994) : 59. Concept by C. S. Lewis.

[2] ——— , "Two-Course Meal," *Delta Kappa Gamma Bulletin* 61, No. 3 (Spring 1995) : 61.

CHAPTER 22

SHE LOOKS LIKE A GOAL-SETTER: "S'IL VOUS PLAÎT, MONSIEUR..."

Your life can't go according to plan if you have no plan.
—Unknown

"Be strong and courageous...
for the Lord your God is with you wherever you go."
—Joshua 1:9, NASB

Queen Esther, Abigail, and Mary Magdalene were all beautiful women who set goals, and then, leaning on the Lord, took incredible risks to attain those goals.

Esther's goal was to save her people from being annihilated at the hand of her royal husband's prime minister. To attain her goal, Esther risked going before King Ahasuerus without being summoned—and was welcomed with the proffered scepter, sparing both her life and, by extention, the lives of her people.

Abigail's goal was to spare the life of her husband, Nabal, and save his vast nomadic estate (1 Sam. 25). The risky strategy she used to attain her goal involved approaching the angered Israelite king-elect, David, to assume the blame for her foolish husband's volatile behavior. As a result, she not only saved her household and estate but also became a queen of Israel herself.

Compared to these two Old Testament queens, Mary Magdalene's goal was simple, but perhaps the most difficult goal of all to achieve. Mary yearned to be pure. But before this miracle could occur, she had to risk baring her sins of immorality to the Saviour, again and again.

Not only was Mary the first person allowed to see Christ after His resurrection, but 2,000 years after the fact she remains a symbol of divine redemption from addictive sin. Christ guaranteed that wherever His story would be told, so would Mary's (John 12).

A beautiful woman sets goals and takes risks to attain those goals.

Downright scary!

Taking risks to reach a goal can be downright scary! From childhood, tales of the exotic told by returned missionaries inspired in me the desire to one day be a missionary in Africa. The young man I married had this identical goal. However, we needed to become literate in French, since our denomination needed secondary teachers for its schools in francophone Africa.

It's one thing to memorize verb conjugations and phrases from *Beginning French Made Easy*, but it's an entirely different matter to risk actually speaking *la belle langue!* Especially *in France*, of all places! Talk about an intimidating risk!

My most memorable faux pas included an argument of sorts with a railroad conductor when he asked for my ticket in a crowded train compartment near Le Havre. I thought I was stating, in my baby French, that I was the wife of the man sitting next to me—my husband, who had my train ticket.

What I was actually saying—and in the informal (a.k.a. disrespectful when speaking to a stranger) pronoun/verb form—was *"Je suis ta femme* ["I am *your* wife"]."

"No, you're not!" answered the conductor in clipped French. *"Votre billet, s'il vous plaît!"* he repeated.

I was doing my best to tell him that my husband had my *billet,* so I once again endeavored to point out the man to whom I was married.

"I am your *wife!"* I insisted more loudly, while the other passengers quietly exchanged raised-eyebrowed glances. My husband, already fluent after a year of language study in French, rescued me.

Although shaken by my failed communication attempt, I risked another plunge into *la belle langue* at a restaurant when we arrived in Paris. Attempting to appear as self-possessed as possible, I asked the stuffy maitre d' for a bottle of ketchup for my *pommes frites.*

"Monsieur, je suis . . . une bouteille de . . . ketchup . . . s'il vous plaît!" I enunciated clearly and loudly.

He nodded and appeared to choke slightly before heading back toward the kitchen.

"So how did I do?" I asked my husband.

"Not too badly," he answered slowly. "The good news is that you used the polite, instead of the informal, form. The bad news is that you just announced to everyone within earshot that *you* are a bottle of ketchup."

"Oh, no!" I moaned, now understanding the amused looks on the faces of those sitting at the nearest table.

"But don't feel too bad," consoled my spouse. "At least you added 'If it pleases you.'"

Risking spoken French that school year in Collonges-sous-Saleve definitely paid off in my becoming at least literate in the language. During the next nine years, by knowing French I was able to shop, write, teach, pray, and—best of all—make friends in French-speaking Africa. Goal achieved! (But I'll spare you my Swahili blunders!)

Why should I worry or . . . *what?*

When setting goals, a beautiful woman realistically assesses her abilities and wisely stays within those limitations.

During premission orientation at Andrews University's excellent Missions Institute, I learned the dangers of overextending one's self in a foreign language. In the area of translation, for example. Earlier this century well-meaning missionaries had attempted to translate English lyrics into African languages. The results were most interesting.

One British hymn has the phrase "Sin dies, simply to rot." When translated into an African dialect by an Englishman it became "It is good for you to rot." Then there was an American missionary who attempted translating the more recent set of lyrics to the gospel song "I Gave My Heart to Jesus; How About You?" Unfortunately, the translated version put this spin on the song: "I Gave My Heart to Jesus—What's the Matter With You?"

OK, so I knew all this and should have left lyrics translation well outside of my risk-taking arena. But no! My relative success in mastering *remedial* French gave me the unrealistic thought that I might do a little translation from English into Kinyarwanda. After all, I had taken a dozen lessons already.

In spite of the fact that I knew about translation pitfalls. In spite of the fact that Kinyarwanda is a tonal language, which makes correct translation of musical lyrics extremely challenging. In spite of the fact that our language teacher carefully instructed us to pronounce certain syllables low so that we would say in Kinyarwanda, "I am coming to your house to visit you," and *not* "I am coming to your house to pass gas."

In spite of *all* these facts I decided, after only a few months of sparse language instruction, that I would translate just one short line of a song. I would do this without the help of the local pastor-translator with whom I had been working closely on previous musical translations. (Up to then I had taken Pastoro the lyrics, and he'd translated them. Then I'd sung every line to him so he could verify if the syllables were appropriately matched with the pitches of the notes, keeping the original meaning intact—and avoiding embarrassing mistranslations.)

The song was uncomplicated. Pastoro had already translated most of it, but I kept that one line for myself. My little secret. That one simple line was repeated four times in every verse and chorus sequence, so my deft translation would have great public exposure. Cool!

Two weeks later, as we performed before a 600-member outdoor camp meeting congregation, I had the distinct pleasure of listening to a full choir sing *my* translated line: "I believe, I believe, I believe, so why should I worry or fret?"

After the service, Pastoro slowly and respectfully approached. Drawing me aside he said, "Madamu, all the songs your group sang in our tongue today touched my heart."

"Well, praise the Lord for that!" I responded, secretly taking too much personal credit for his spiritual blessing.

"I am confused, however, by that repeated line in the last song you sang," he continued.

Well, you can imagine which line it was—the line I'd translated all by my egotistical lonesome.

"Would you be kind enough," Pastoro requested, "to sing that line for me again so that I can understand it better?"

I obliged by singing in my very best newly acquired Kinyarwanda: "I believe, so why should I worry or fret?"

He listened. Then looking up into the rustling eucalyptus trees for a long moment, the old pastor, who'd dealt for more than 60 years with idealistic young missionaries, took a deep breath. Gently—very gently—he explained that what I had actually translated, and what the accommodating college chorale had just publicly sung, was "I believe, I believe, I believe, so why should I throw up all the time?"

What are your goals?

What are your goals? God's goals for us are more than we can even imagine, if we give Him full control. Four and a half years ago my principal sent me to a three-day seminar on how to set up a self-esteem program in our school. The conference facilitators focused on personal self-esteem as well as schoolwide self-esteem. In one of the sessions we participants were given 10 minutes to draw up a list of goals we would like to achieve in the next 20 years. We were to give no consideration to financial constraints, societal limitations, or any lack of physical or intellectual abilities we might have. At the end of 10 minutes we were paired with a partner and shared our list of goals, as if we had already accomplished them, role-playing that we were classmates at our 20-year high school reunion.

My goals included accomplishments such as learning to speak fluent Spanish, getting a Ph.D. in English, losing 10 pounds, teaching on the university level before I retired, owning and learning to play a Dobro, being rich enough to be a homeowner (talk about dreaming the impossible dream!), playing backup banjo in a bluegrass band, living in a mountain cabin with a porch large enough for a rocking chair and hound dog (and from which we could all enjoy the spectacular view of the sun setting over Mount Shasta). Among other items, I wrote (tongue-in-cheek) that I would someday have enough income for groceries—and no responsibilities except to cross-country ski and write poetry and children's stories all day long. But I especially wanted to earn enough money to fund whatever branch of higher education my son chose to follow.

After the exercise at the conference, I couldn't put the list out of my mind. So much of it was so purely selfish that I laughed at myself. But before I went to bed that night I remembered God telling Abraham to dream big, to visualize his descendants as the sands of the sea and the stars of the heavens. God said to look out across the landscape and visualize—as far as Abraham could see—his descendants owning all that real estate. God's goals for Abraham, if rightly achieved and prayerfully maintained, were to be for Heaven's glory.

Jesus told His followers, "Seek ye first the kingdom of God" (Matt. 6:33). Then would follow some of the other stuff. Before I went to bed that night I pulled out my list, confessed my selfishness and doubt, gave God permission to bring—or not to bring—any of it to pass, and went on about my life.

As I said, that was four and a half years ago. Today, however, a quick mental check of the list, which I put on a back burner, forces me to catch my breath and marvel at how the God who told Abraham to dream big has offered me nearly all the options I wrote down that day in the seminar. I am also humbled that on most items God has respected me enough to leave the final decisions up to *me!* (I'll share more particulars a little later.)

Risking presumption

Laying my wish list before God was a frightening experience, in a way. I didn't want to be presumptuous, like the little girl whose penny-counting parents were finally able to afford taking her to a restaurant for the first time. The child was especially impressed by the attendant who brought her everything she asked for.

After putting on her pajamas that evening, she appeared in the living room with a writing tablet and pencil.

"OK," she announced, "it's time for my good-night prayer. Now who wants what?"[1]

On the other hand, John informs us that if we pray according to God's will, He hears us (1 John 5:14, 15). But how can we *know* God's will in order to pray according to it?

I believe the secret to successful, *Spirit-led* goal setting and risk taking is getting to *know* God by spending as much time as possible with Him—anytime, anywhere: at home during personal devotions, on ski slopes, in church, at a concert, alone, while eating popcorn with friends, while eating out, waiting for the traffic light to change, when you're angry, and when you're in love.

Having recently moved across country, I've started again from square one as far as making—and getting to know—new friends. Unless I eat lunch with them, exercise with them, worship with them, celebrate birthdays with them, listen to them, see how they react when I am needy . . . *unless I spend time with them, I won't know them—ever.*

Likewise, if I don't spend abundant amounts of time with God, I won't ever know the heart of God or how to pray according to His will. That's why Jesus said, "Seek ye first the kingdom of God, and his righteousness; and all these things will be added unto you" (Matt. 6:33).

W. Bingham Hunter, who has done much biblical research on prayer, draws this conclusion: "I passionately disagree with the notion that prayer is a way to get from God what we want. Christian prayer, as explained in Scripture, seems something else entirely: *Prayer is a means God uses to give us what He wants.*"[2]

After the fact

About the goals on The List. God began gradually revealing His will to me. I do *not* own a rude log cabin on a mountainside with a front-porch view of Mount Shasta, which I enjoy each evening with my hound dog. Nor do I own the hound dog, along with all its fleas. I do *not* have at my selfish disposal balmy days in which to hike beckoning trails, cross-country ski, and watch bird migrations through binoculars. For a time God allowed me to pursue some of my other listed goals, then brought me to points of decision—mine.

The following autumn, when the Spanish teacher at my school invited me, out of the blue, to join her community college evening Spanish class, I thought, *Whoa, Lord! No kidding! I told You I wanted to speak Spanish.* But six weeks later I reluctantly withdrew—and never registered. My late-night study of *Español* was adversely affecting my own teaching performance and slowing down my students' paper corrections.

While studying on a humanities grant at the University of Arkansas one summer, two years after I'd listed my goals, my professor (out of the blue, again) asked if I'd ever considered getting a Ph.D. Remembering The List, I sat bolt upright and said yes, but also mentioned I didn't know how I could finance such a project and still support myself.

"Based on what you've been doing in our seminar," he offered, "I'd be willing to do anything I could to make this possible for you—including a letter of recommendation and helping you obtain a teaching assistantship. Then you could just about support yourself through the degree program."

Not knowing the will of God in this matter, I decided to "walk down the hallway" for the next year and let Him open or shut the doors as I came to them. I passed the Graduate Record Examination, obtained positive recommendation letters, was accepted as a candidate into the doctoral program of the English Department, and secured an apartment in student housing on the campus.

Then, just at the time when I'd be needing to make a final decision about whether I was really going to commit the next three years of my energy, time, and finances to an all-out push for a Ph.D., someone phoned me from Oregon and invited me to look over a teaching position there. *Oregon!* I didn't even *know* anyone in Oregon. Why would I want to move up there?

Goals attained

The following year, the year that I lived in breathtakingly beautiful Oregon, was the most peaceful time I'd had in years. Not only did my new colleagues and students contribute abundantly to my spiritual and professional growth, but also I *loved* the hiking, bird-watching, cross-country skiing, and the Rogue River rafting opportunities this new area afforded me. I especially enjoyed sitting on the front stoop of my rental apartment at dusk and looking at the mountain that rose on the other side of Interstate 5. My first two months there I prayed, "If it is Your will, Lord, it is certainly mine to live in Oregon until Your second coming! And if it makes any difference to You, I really, really, *really* hope it is Your will."

Today, 12 months after I began praying *that* prayer, I write these words from the upstairs study of a small townhouse in the state of Maryland—the brand-new townhouse in which the *will of God* has placed this single, financially challenged woman. As owner. You see, after a series of lightning-quick events (divinely ordained, I have no doubt!) over the course of a nine-month school year, I ended up loving—and tearfully leaving—my newly known students and church family.

Moving 3,000 miles away from family and friends, I am still in youth ministry and, at the same time, being paid to work with writing! I own a Dobro and was once paid for playing my banjo in public. With incomprehensible magnanimity, God has brought to fruition the most outlandish, unrealistic goals on The List—though I'll never understand why. At this point I am as overwhelmed and as grateful as a human being can be.

Taking nothing for granted

However, through the synchronizing of my list of goals with God's list of goals, I have been learning to take nothing for granted. I take the joy as well as the growth in each 24-hour period. One of God's future goals for me may land me in the outback of Tasmania doing missionary work. Or perhaps three years from now I might best follow His will sharing His good news with a fellow patient in some hospital cancer ward.

On a daily basis I await the unfolding of His will.

"Seek ye first the kingdom of God," Jesus counseled. A beautiful woman may not always know where God's goals are leading her. But she *can* know that when her goals and God's goals for her become the same, any risks she takes toward achieving them will be the safest risks she ever took!

---

[1] P. Susan and Steven R. Mamchak, eds., *Encyclopedia of School Humor* (West Nyack, N.Y.: Parker Pub. Co., Inc., 1987), p. 182.

[2] W. B. Hunter, *The God Who Hears,* p. 12.

CHAPTER 23

SHE LOOKS TEACHABLE: A LESSON FROM THE LAMB

He was pierced through for our transgressions . . . and
like a sheep that is silent before its shearers, so He did not open His mouth.
—Isaiah 53:5-7, NASB

Since before the day God calmed Moses' butterflies about becoming a public speaker with the words "I will be with thy mouth" (Ex. 4:15), God has portrayed Himself as an able teacher. The teachable, such as King David ("Guide me in your truth and teach me" [Psalm 25:4, 5, NIV]), have been willing to listen, observe, and learn.

Jesus, the Lamb of God, was first a learner at His mother's knee before becoming a teacher—on the hillsides, beside the Sea of Galilee, in the synagogues—tirelessly opening His listeners' minds and hearts to ever-increasing knowledge about the Father. Followers called Him Teacher, and those who believed admitted, "You teach the way of God" (Mark 12:14, NIV).

For three and a half years He practiced what He taught. But history remembers His most memorable lesson as being on the day when He said the least, the day He modeled heaven's sacrificial love while hanging—and dying—in near-complete silence on a cross. The teachable among those present in Calvary's "classroom" learned a lesson that changed their lives.

Nearly 2,000 years later the Lord continues to adapt His lessons of love to meet the needs and understanding of the assorted students coming together in His most unlikely "classrooms."

Fang wounds

In the far corner of the veranda slumped a large sheep. The dirty, matted wool on its chest was slowly absorbing the blood that streamed from bite tears in its flesh. The sheep's owner, glowering darkly and muttering clipped sinister oaths in Swahili, stood above his animal. His cronies from the local Congolese village nodded in agreement.

"And they call themselves missionaries," said one, spitting over the back wall. "Yet they let their dogs attack our sheep."

"Where were they, anyway, when it happened?" asked another man, pointing at me with his chin.

"They were in church," one of the men replied caustically.

"You can bet they will pay dearly for this," intoned the sheep's owner. "This is my family's only sheep." He emphasized his point by roughly nudging the sheep with his bare foot. The creature moaned.

"Why this, God?" I lamented, knowing well how a touchy incident such as this could seriously damage the effectiveness of our ministry. "Why now, when we're finally starting to feel at home here?" In the near corner of the veranda cowered Christy, our German shepherd.

In our mid-20s my husband and I lived halfway around the world from our families. Doing our lonely best to adapt to a developing country's culture, we had taken comfort in the warmth and companionship of our little German shepherd pup, having obtained her from the Ugandan police kennels on our way into the Congo the year before. Christy had never attacked another animal before. I was certain she had only wanted to play with the hapless ewe.

Now guttural groans punctuated the sheep's labored breathing. Involuntarily, I glanced at the sickening sight in the far corner.

Nightmare on the veranda

Noon sunshine reflected off the broad banana leaves waving lazily in the plantation breeze. We had just returned from a service in the school chapel. How precious had been those moments of Easter worship with our African brothers and sisters. God had seemed so close as we knelt before Him in praise and thanksgiving for the priceless sacrifice of His Son, the gift that united races and cultures. With comforted spirits we had left that place of renewal, only to walk down the hill into the nightmare unfolding on our back veranda.

Even in a nontechnological society bad news travels fast. Soon passersby on the road, home from market, wandered into the yard to find out the reason for the gathering crowd. A young woman in a bright wraparound *pagne*, balancing a bottle of palm oil on her head, asked the sheep's owner what had happened. He didn't hesitate to tell her. A wrinkled little woman, holding two upside-down chickens by their feet, cackled through her toothless grin as the chickens clucked miserably. More and more curious sightseers clumped together in chattering groups, craning their necks to view the proceedings on our veranda. By threes and fours, students who had finished their lunch in the school dining area approached. They waited respectfully on the lawn, where they could be within hearing distance.

All, that is, except Eliel, a natural-born leader who had instigated three student strikes already this year. I recognized his loud laugh even before he emerged from the banana plantation. Brazenly he led three of his peers onto the back porch without first asking permission to approach, as was the local custom. I was offended by their poorly disguised excitement and glee at our predicament.

"Where is your husband, madamu?" Eliel bluntly demanded, as if he were taking control of the situation. His friends stepped closer to hear my soft answer.

"He took the car to get Nurse Solomon from the dispensary," I answered carefully, feeling more alone than ever.

"Is a nurse for *people* going to tend to an *animal?*" Eliel asked, scarcely concealing his amusement.

Nurse Solomon

Just then the roar of our Peugeot's unmuffled exhaust pipe announced Nurse Solomon's arrival. He sat in the front passenger seat next to my pale-faced husband. Some onlookers in the yard tittered as Solomon pushed his way through them, black instrument bag clutched tightly in his hand, a no-nonsense look on his kind African face.

"What are you going to do, Nurse Solomon?" demanded the sheep's owner.

"I am going to sew up the wounds on your sheep," answered Solomon quietly, ignoring Eliel's loud laugh.

"Lift your animal up on this table, please."

"Why bother?" countered the owner. "My animal is going to die. I just want money so I can replace it, that's all."

"This sheep is far from being dead," insisted Solomon, "so put it on the table."

I feared the owner would turn violent, he looked so angry. But after a long, dangerous silence he exhaled loudly and motioned a villager standing next to him to help lift the sheep onto the Ping-Pong table.

Solomon gently bound the suffering creature's legs. Feeling like a moth caught in a spider's web, I had no choice but to watch helplessly what was taking place. As Solomon removed a large half-moon needle from his black bag and started threading it, onlookers' excited exchanges faded abruptly. Silently Solomon disinfected a ragged wound near the sheep's throat. Even the sheep's owner had stopped his muttering to watch. My stomach tightened even more.

God, where are You? What good can possibly come of this? And Easter! Of all weekends, I complained silently. This was downright unfair! Had I not been so emotionally spent, I would have felt anger.

With a determined thrust Solomon jabbed the needle through the animal's raw flesh. I cringed, anticipating a cry of pain. It didn't come. Instead I heard a sympathetic grunt or two from Eliel's group. Thirty minutes passed as Nurse Solomon repeatedly pressed the needle into the animal's flesh. He deftly secured each stitch with a neat, tiny knot.

An hour went by. Realizing that this surgical procedure was bound to be a long, monotonous one, the marketgoers began losing interest in the drama and wandered off to pick up the thread of their daily lives. By now the owner seemed resigned to the fact that his sheep was in competent hands.

But even though the sheep's owner had stopped his grumbling, I wasn't finished with mine. Feeling shortchanged by God, I leaned against my husband's shoulder, listlessly observing the scene.

It just doesn't make sense, I whimpered inwardly, swiping at a large fly buzzing about my face.

I beg your pardon

I slowly became aware that nearly everyone except the sheep's owner—and Eliel, of all people—had slipped away. Eliel was standing near Solomon's elbow now. I did remember that in one of my classes he had expressed an interest in medicine.

"The sheep never cried," he commented unexpectedly to no one in particular.

"I beg your pardon," I said dully, as Solomon rethreaded the now-blunt needle.

Eliel glanced up at me as if his train of thought had been interrupted. "Oh, I was just noticing how patient the sheep is," he sort of mumbled.

It was then that I realized that Eliel had been watching the sheep, not Solomon. He turned his gaze on the creature again, and for once the proud, self-confident Eliel had nothing to say.

"How *is* the sheep?" my husband asked Solomon in English.

"She'll be fine if the owner keeps her wounds clean," he answered, and began to unbind her legs.

Well, the worst was over. I must admit I was still smarting from the sting of public humiliation. Solomon gently lifted the sheep down from the table and set it gingerly on its unsteady feet, all the while giving instructions for its care to the owner. The owner nodded. Then Solomon clicked his black bag shut and slid onto the front seat of the car again. The Peugeot loudly disappeared in the direction of the dispensary, farther up the mountain.

Down the path through the banana plantation the injured sheep dutifully plodded after its master. Eliel, the only person on the veranda now besides myself, watched them disappear around a bend through the lush foliage. He just kept standing there on the top step, looking at the spot where they'd been hidden from view.

I waited for a moment or two and then asked cautiously, "Eliel? Are you all right?"

Hanging his head, he slowly turned and met my questioning gaze.

He seemed oblivious to my question.

"Did you see how that creature just lay there?" he asked. "No struggling. Hardly any groaning, though I know it was in pain . . ." He stopped and swallowed hard before continuing. His eyes had a moist, troubled look to them. "Remember when they read in church today that Jesus was led like a lamb to be slaughtered . . . and He didn't even open His mouth to cry? I heard that in church once before but didn't really understand that Jesus *chose* . . . to suffer . . . like that lamb . . . for me."

Now it was *my* turn to hang my head, because I'd heard it in church *all my life* and was just now realizing that perhaps I hadn't really understood either.

For one silent, hallowed moment we stood—a proud Congolese teenager and a young missionary of little faith—unexpectedly touched, softened, and united by a lesson from the Lamb.

CHAPTER 24

SHE LOOKS LOVED: EVERYBODY LOVES A LOVER —DON'T THEY?

*F*ew women have experienced the kind of loyal love the wayward Gomer received from the minor prophet Hosea. "I will betroth you to Me forever; yes, I will betroth you to Me in righteousness and in justice, in lovingkindness and in compassion, and I will betroth you to Me in faithfulness" (Hosea 2:19, 20, NASB). The self-sacrifice exhibited by Hosea as he waited for Gomer to turn her heart back toward him, the longing he felt for her, seem almost too overwhelming to have been reality.

God's proclamations of love for His chosen people in the writings of the Old Testament prophets are also proclamations of His love for you, beautiful and valuable woman. He patiently waits to clothe, bejewel, and nourish *you* from the abundance of His love. Perhaps you have often kept Him waiting (as I have) as He patiently waits for the gift of a *whole* heart instead of getting it piecemeal.

Have you ever known anyone so in love (unrequited) that disappointment after disappointment failed to discourage them? I have.

Yobu, man of sorrows

A persistent clearing of the throat and a courteous cough brought me to the front door of my home at Gitwe College in Rwanda.

"Madamu, I have come to ask for your daughter's hand in marriage," said the elderly African, bowing politely.

My eyes swept over him, taking in the gray-bordered bald spot on the top of his shiny head, the dust-colored tatters he wore, and the weathered feet, each missing a toe or two. His request confused me.

"But I have no daughter," I responded.

"Ah, but you do," he patiently insisted. "You know—your *daughter*," he emphasized, gesturing past my shoulder in the direction of the doorway through which a song was wafting. The singer was the lovely, 16-year-old, soft-skinned Yosefina who, in addition to helping me with daily cooking and chores, had become a close friend. I understood.

"But you must make marriage arrangements with her father," I explained unnecessarily.

"*N'ibyo koko,* this is true, madamu, but I need her first to turn her heart toward me." He squinted through cataract-filmed eyes.

"And to whom am I speaking?" I asked the peculiar little man.

"To Yobu. Job, man of many sorrows," he answered with a gallant bow of his head. Then he smiled a great vacant grin, revealing black space where his front two teeth had once been. I smiled back.

"Help me with Yosefina," he pleaded. Then he bowed slightly and shuffled off.

Who is Yobu?

"All right, I've got to know," I said, hurrying out to the back porch, where Yosefina was hanging up newly washed clothes. "Who is Yobu?"

She met my innocent question with a burst of laughter and a 15-minute chronicle of Yobu's past, punctuated by animated bits of information supplied by Samueli, weeding in the pineapple patch.

As a young man Yobu had been engaged to a pretty girl of his tribe. But sometime during the prenuptial celebrations with his age-mates one of Yobu's defeated rivals in love, still nursing a grudge, spiked Yobu's mug of *urwagwa* with poison. Yobu became gravely ill, hovering for days between life and death.

He not only missed his own wedding, but also no longer had full use of his mental faculties when he recovered. In fact many people in these hills referred to him as *musazi,* the crazy one. Since that sad day he had fancied himself a youthful, if not debonair, suitor, always on the verge of winning the affections of some young, nubile thing.

"The girls he first courted are old women now!" laughed Samueli.

It seems that Yobu managed a meager subsistence by doing chores, such as chopping wood, usually for the father of some marriageable daughter. He was a familiar figure at dowry ceremonies and wedding feasts, drinking long draughts of *urwagwa* through a bamboo straw thrust deep into the communal earthen pot. Then he would sit back and eye the bridal attendants, flirting with his eyebrows and making comical nodding movements with his head.

This week his eyes were on Yosefina. Beween spells of giggling, she recounted how Yobu was visiting her father almost daily, declaring his love, bargaining for a dowry, and offering to wait until Yosefina was ready—a veritable Jacob negotiating for his Rachel.

Letdown

Eleven months later Yosefina's father gave her in marriage—but not to Yobu. Rather, she married a straight-backed, suit-clad young businessman with a handsome jawline and an equally handsome dowry.

Yobu was devastated. For the next week he shuffled, stiff-kneed, to my front door, daily mourning his loss of Yosefina and gently reprimanding me for not having more strongly encouraged her to see his finer qualities.

The week after, however, his shuffling step became lighter, and he confided he'd found a new fiancée—the buxom, doe-eyed daughter of a local deacon. Yobu asked me to intercede with my *bwana* to find him a pair of shoes and a necktie in which to go courting. Good-naturedly my husband complied, knowing full well that the forgetful Yobu would probably not be able to relocate these items once he took them off.

"My wedding feast will be soon," he assured me. "She will turn her heart toward me."

But when the deacon's daughter told Yobu two months later she was engaged to someone else, he patiently began working to earn a dowry for the accountant's daughter. And when *she* became someone else's fiancée, Yobu was back to square one, foraging in the woods for kindling. Not for himself, of course. No, for with a constant supply of kindling perhaps the local church field president and his wife, who had two daughters of marriageable age, would look kindly upon him. In his comings and goings Yobu would often cough politely outside my door and bring me up-to-date on his latest amorous agenda.

"This one, I *know*, will turn her heart toward me," he would say, and then beam.

A peculiar friendship, ours. Yobu began addressing me affectionately as "Mama," although the little, leathery man was twice my age. During visits he occasionally requested a shirt, a jacket, or a watch to complete the outfit he said he would wear to his upcoming wedding feast. I gave him what I could, always with a loaf of fresh bread. Yobu would grin that great vacant grin of his, and we would both feel just a bit richer.

And that's how Yobu and his never-ending quest for a bride became part of the warp and woof that made up my first five years on Gitwe Hill in Rwanda.

A new hope

One busy morning a clearing of a throat and the now-familiar shallow cough announced Yobu's presence on the front porch. Between his hands he clutched a small bunch of bananas. Holding out the gift, Yobu stated simply, "Mama, I have come to ask for your daughter's hand in marriage. May I have her, please?"

It took a minute before Yobu's request sank in. As he grinned expectantly, Perusi, Yosefina's plump, 18-year-old replacement, stepped into the living room with a question. Seeing Yobu, she giggled and quickly darted back into the kitchen.

"Oh, Yobu" was all I could say. A great sadness came over me, for I knew that even if I possessed the persuasive skills of an expert matchmaker along with all the arrows in Cupid's quiver, I would never be able to fulfill his deepest desire.

"The question of marriage, Yobu, Perusi will have to answer for herself," I answered evasively.

"But, Mama," he pleaded in his honeyed-gravel voice, "I think perhaps you can help her turn her heart toward me."

Heartbreak

My final morning on Gitwe Hill was one of bustle, of last-minute packing, of pretending my heart wouldn't break the next time another red-eyed friend came to bid farewell.

Then I heard it—the distinct clearing of the throat, the courteous little cough. He stood in the doorway, the same tatter-clad caricature of humanity that had first visited me six years before. For a moment I could not speak as my mind raced over the most recent turbulent events in Yobu's futile pursuit for the heart of a bride.

Alas, the bubbly Perusi had loved another instead of him, had become pregnant out of wedlock, and had gone off discreetly to the city to give birth. The afternoon this news became public property, Yobu had shuffled straight to my house. Going directly to the back porch he, a defeated suitor once again, had confronted me from the other side of the washtub over which I was bending, soapsuds clinging to my elbows.

This time he felt doubly betrayed, and misery etched even more deeply the many lines on his weary face. "You didn't help me make her turn her heart toward me," he moaned accusingly, "and now she has given herself to another. How *could* you have let this happen?"

Together we grieved, for Perusi had become like a little sister to me, and I knew the choice she had made guaranteed destitution for her baby and herself. I sent Yobu off with a fresh loaf of bread, which would at least warm his stomach. I could do nothing for his heart.

Now, on my last day on Gitwe Hill, he stood before me, a liter can of dried beans between his hands. "For you, Mama," he said softly, holding it out with both hands. "It might be planting season when you get back to America, and you won't have any seeds in your field from the last harvest. What will you and your family eat if you don't have these?"

I managed to choke out a "God bless you" before he took up his mournful refrain: "She didn't turn her heart toward me! Oh, she didn't! How I suffer . . . but perhaps God will yet find me a bride. Don't you think so?"

I put down the can of beans.

"Oh, my friend of many sorrows," I said, grasping one of his leathery hands with both of mine, "that's what I will pray for you."

He smiled his sad, vacant smile.

"Go with God," he said in the form of a blessing, both his hands now over mine. He slowly released them, took his walking stick from where it leaned against the wall, and shuffled up the walk—and out of my life.

The patient bridegroom

Like Yobu, God patiently waits for His daughters to turn even the most protected parts of their hearts toward Him. He waits for them to understand just how beautiful they are.

" 'With great compassion I will gather you. . . . With everlasting lovingkindness I will have compassion on you,' Says the Lord your Redeemer" (Isa. 54:7, 8, NASB).

With the patience of Yobu, the heavenly Bridegroom waits for each of us to brush-stroke warm colors into her portrait, painting with the confidence of someone who knows she is loved . . . without measure.

CHAPTER 25

SHE LOOKS . . .
LIKE A LEADING LADY

Opening Night

(December 1967)

I stand tall,
surrounded by bridesmaids in blue velvet,
arranging a pearl-scattered veil
across my white taffeta'd shoulders.
In the bustling bridal room
I stand,
nervously anticipating
this opening night,
this eve of a lifetime.

❦ ❦ ❦

(December 1993)

I stand tall (again, I think),
prompter's scripts at my feet,
and pull an old woolen jacket
about my weary shoulders.
On this empty set
I stand
under the dimming stagelights
at the end of this,
another opening night.
—Carolyn Rathbun

*H*andsome knight! It is I, fair maiden, trapped on yon dungeon balcony. I shall leap behind thee upon thy snow-white steed. Stayest thou there and let us ride off together!

OK. Jump hard enough to clear the oleander bush. One—two—three—go!
Ouch, handsome knight! That branch hath scratched my leg. Oh, no—
I'm losing my balance.

Gentle knight, I have underleaped, missed thy steed, and fallen to the
ground. Pray thee, canst thou patiently hold on a minute and let me have
another shot at it?

But the fair maiden didn't have enough time to leap again from the
white clapboard porch, because the music teacher opened the door to
let me know my brother's piano lesson was over. It was my turn now.
Casting a sidelong glance at the invisible knight waiting patiently for me
at the base of the oleander bush, I reluctantly closed another chapter in
my imaginary story. Picking up John Schirmer's *Intermediate Études*, I
dutifully followed the demanding but doting Mrs. Werner to the hard
bench at the shiny grand piano dominating her sterile parlor.

The sneak reading of a library book fairy tale a couple days before had
launched my 7-year-old fertile imagination onto crusades of its own.
Currently I was despising the fact that my untimely birth had been in the
twentieth century instead of during the Middle Ages. But more than that,
I resented the fact that my parents hadn't brought me into the world as a
boy who could actually *become* a knight, had he lived in the "olden days."

But alas and alack! Being most definitely a girl, I had to choose the
next-best paradigm for the self-protagonist in my imaginary scenarios.
So I had become a fair maiden—but one who, most assuredly, could *do*
everything a knight could!

Role models

Aristotle suggested that looking to good role models and imitating
their choices will lead to living a good life. Greek theater offered a variety of characters. Through them the audience could vicariously make
ethical choices, evaluate the consequences, and then go home and hopefully make sound decisions, based on their models.

What a variety of models one has from which to choose! I'll never
forget a conversation I once had returning from a date one Saturday
night during college years. My young escort, whose father had recently
shot himself, disclosed to me a model that was helping him to cope with
his monumental loss, a model who was giving him the hope and courage
to go on. I was dumbfounded to learn that this model wasn't even a real
person! It was the character Molly Brown from the musical play *The
Unsinkable Molly Brown.*

When I told my date I hadn't seen the play, he explained that when
calamity after calamity hit Molly Brown, she always chose to "resurface."

"Carolyn," he said with deep emotion in his voice, "I am going to
be like Molly Brown." And with his role model's determination my
friend became a blessing to countless people as a medical doctor.

Choosing our models

I suppose I was not the only little girl to pattern at least parts of her life after story characters, both real and imaginary. Jo in *Little Women* taught me that one can live in poverty and still experience priceless riches in terms of imagination and family love.

Even though my parents didn't know I'd read the story, "Cinderella" taught me that even when ugly stepsisters say *I'm* ugly, the beauty is still in there somewhere, waiting to surprise me.

From Queen Esther I learned that God may think that you or I, out of all the people on earth, may be the best person for a job.

Joseph helped me understand there are no balconies in dungeons, and that the way back out can take a long time.

Jane Eyre underscored the importance of giving extra care to a child from a broken home and transforming love to someone who may not have ever given it to anyone else.

Portia, from Shakespeare's *The Merchant of Venice,* taught me that a woman of moral courage *can* become her own person in a man's world.

Dorcas, with her quiet, consistent care for the poor, taught me that even if I can't change the world, I can make a world of difference to somebody.

And although I don't consider them proper role models, characters such as Queen Jezebel and Lady Macbeth are continual reminders that one intentionally harbored sin (such as pride, the need to control, or lust) can be a gently angeled on-ramp to the highway that ends in hell.

All these characters, real or imaginary, have been role models and actors on my earthly stage. In *As You Like It* Shakespeare wrote, "All the world's a stage." Each of us is the lead actor in her personal play, the central subject of her own life story—the leading lady, if you please.

Acting lessons

Jesus wants to be your director and coach. Although He won't be pushy about it, He loves nothing better than for you to ask Him for coaching sessions. He loves to see you take up your script, your "learn-to-paint" manual, to study and memorize it while awaiting His expert pointers for each scene in which you must play your part. He knows what will work best for your particular role because, you see, He played that very part on this same stage 2,000 years ago.

The Ultimate Art Show

Few things during my teaching were as rewarding as seeing my fifth and sixth graders, after weeks of preholiday rehearsals, coaching sessions, inter-actor ego altercations, and dress rehearsals, throw caution to the wind and act their hearts out during the Christmas program. What pride and joy they brought to their parents!

I suspect that after *your* performance on this world's stage is finished, one of the greatest joys for the Saviour, the Director, Coach, and Master Artist, will be to give you a guided tour of His Ultimate Art Show.

You know, don't you, how amusing patients look coming out of an optometrist's office after they've had their pupils dilated for the glaucoma test? They have to go out in public wearing those thin plastic wraparound shades until their eyes can handle normal light again. Well, I imagine that the first view of Jesus will make one wish she had those shades until her eyes can adjust to the brilliance of His presence.

I hope you don't mind if I come along as He escorts you past several exhibit rooms in His Galaxy Gallery, and then through a multicolored portico designating the entry into the Hall of Beauty.

"The most striking section of this hall," the Master will explain, "is known as the 'Corridor of Leading Ladies.' I'll take you there first."

We round a corner and find ourselves at the beginning of a seemingly endless hall lined by two high walls of transparent marble. Along both walls, as if floating in the air, are portraits of the most exquisite women we have ever seen.

To the right, a woman with thick cascades of wavy chestnut hair gazes down upon us from her portrait. Something about her guileless eyes resembles the pure gaze of the Saviour's. The plaque at the base of the frame reads "Mary Magdalene—A Perfect Likeness."

Across from that portrait, a silver frame outlines some wonderful woman of wisdom, a smile playing about her full, rosy lips. This portrait is entitled "Sarah, Woman of Faith and Mother of Millions—A Perfect Likeness." The set of her finely-chiseled chin is so much like the Master's.

We walk slowly down the corridor and gaze. Actually, I'm not gazing—I'm staring unabashedly at the lovely woman with a smile kind enough to melt your heart. She's Dorcas, another "Perfect Likeness."

Then there's "Naomi—A Perfect Likeness." And, of course, Abigail. Oh and—wow! Eve.

I can tell the Master Artist has been enjoying our astonishment and surprise. He turns and says, "If you think these paintings were brilliantly and laboriously crafted, just wait until you see our newest addition. You're just in time for the unveiling."

We stand at the foot of a large frame draped in satin light through which ripple muted colors of an iridescent rainbow. The Lord gives a slight tug to the corner of the drape and it floats silently to the marble floor. We stand in awed silence.

"My leading lady," He says simply, eloquently, His voice full of emotion. He shakes His head before continuing. "I risked everything for her, and she eventually did the same for Me. What a job we did together on her portrait!"

I squeeze my eyelids against the brilliance and power of this—this masterpiece! It has captured the nearly intimidating magnificence of the most beautiful woman I have ever seen. Its glory literally draws me into this most individual, most original, but closest resemblance to the Master yet, and I am moved to tears. My glance at His beautiful face quickly takes in the tears coursing down His cheeks as well. I can only manage to whisper, "I see why You love her so much."

After a short eternity (for the Curator of the Ultimate Art Show is never in a hurry) I reluctantly pull my eyes from the flawless face in the portrait to look at the identification plate beneath it.

There, engraved on a delicate plate of pure gold, is *your* name. And following that is the inscription: "A Perfect Likeness."

Life Can Be Good

Come and join Christian women who are living life to the fullest. They are building relationships, nurturing family, and finding meaning in their work.

This fresh, new magazine introduces you to intriguing people who share true stories of what God is doing in their lives, and is waiting to do in yours.

Women of Spirit is honest about the challenges facing Christian women, but it's also generous with solutions. Subscribe today and you'll open a door into the abundant life that God intends for you.

One year, six issues, for US$16.95.*

Send check or money order to: *Women of Spirit*, 55 West Oak Ridge Drive, Hagerstown, MD 21740. Please add US$5.10 postage for addresses outside the U.S.A.

Phone orders, call toll-free 1-800-765-6955.

*Price subject to change.

March/April 1997

WOMEN of Spirit
A MAGAZINE OF PRACTICAL CHRISTIANITY

HELPING GOD OUT

Kelli Williams
Captivated by the Love of God

OUTSIDE OF THE INNER CIRCLE

How to Get More From Your Marriage